110909

D0492929

Learning Resource Services: Coleg Powys

002780

# MUSSOLINI AND THE RISE OF FASCISM

By the same author

*The Strategy of the Italian Communist Party*
*Contemporary Italy: Politics, Economy and Society Since 1945*
*One Hundred Years of Socialism*
*Mona Lisa: The History of the World's Most Famous Painting*
*The Culture of the Europeans: From 1800 to the Present*

DONALD SASSOON

# *Mussolini and the*
# *Rise of Fascism*

Harper*Press*
*An Imprint of* HarperCollins*Publishers*

HarperCollins*Publishers*
77–85 Fulham Palace Road,
Hammersmith, London W6 8JB
www.harpercollins.co.uk

Published by HarperCollins*Publishers* 2007

1

Copyright © Donald Sassoon 2007

The author asserts the moral right to
be identified as the author of this work

Maps © HarperCollins*Publishers*, designed by
Two Dot Media

A catalogue record for this book
is available from the British Library

ISBN 978-0-00-719242-7

Set in Linotype Minion by Rowland Phototypesetting Ltd,
Bury St Edmunds, Suffolk

Printed and bound in Great Britain by Clays Ltd, St Ives plc

**Mixed Sources**
Product group from well-managed
forests and other controlled sources
www.fsc.org  Cert no. SW-COC-1806
© 1996 Forest Stewardship Council

FSC is a non-profit international organisation established to promote the
responsible management of the world's forests. Products carrying the FSC
label are independently certified to assure consumers that they come
from forests that are managed to meet the social, economic and
ecological needs of present and future generations.

Find out more about HarperCollins and the environment at
**www.harpercollins.co.uk/green**

All rights reserved. No part of this publication may be
reproduced, stored in a retrieval system, or transmitted,
in any form or by any means, electronic, mechanical,
photocopying, recording or otherwise, without the
prior permission of the publishers.

# CONTENTS

LIST OF MAPS                                    6

LIST OF ILLUSTRATIONS                           7

1  *The Conjuncture*                            9
2  *A Divisive War – a Lost Victory*           31
3  *The Parliamentary Crisis*                  61
4  *The Advance of Fascism*                    89
5  *'We Need a Strong Government'*            120

NOTES                                         145
BIBLIOGRAPHY OF WORKS CITED                   163
INDEX                                         173

# MAPS

Italy's north-eastern border, 1915 and post 1919–20    39

Fiume and surrounding territories    53

Areas of fascist violence between 1920 and 1922    99

# ILLUSTRATIONS

The battle of Asiago, in May 1916, was the only battle in which Mussolini took part. *(Robert Hunt Library)*

Corporal Mussolini, 1917. *(Gettyimages/Time Life)*

Italian troops camping on Mount Pasubio, the main Italian strategic position from 1916 to the end of the war. *(Author's collection)*

Antonio Salandra. *(Gettyimages/Hulton Archive)*

Mussolini's *Il Popolo d'Italia* welcomed Italy's declaration of war on Austria-Hungary. *(Author's collection)*

*Il Popolo d'Italia* prematurely announces victory. *(Author's collection)*

Italian troops in retreat after the devastating defeat at Caporetto in October 1916. *(Corbis /Hulton-Deutsch Collection)*

Mussolini launches the fascist movement in 1919. *(Ullstein Bild)*

Pope Benedict XV. *(Ullstein Bild)*

Francesco Nitti. *(SV-Bilderdienst)*

Gabriele D'Annunzio. *(Corbis/Bettman)*

Large crowds in Fiume celebrate their 'liberation' by D'Annunzio's legionnaires in 1919. *(Corbis/Alinari Archives)*

Mussolini and D'Annunzio in 1935. *(SV-Bilderdienst)*

Lloyd George, Orlando, Clemenceau and Wilson at the Versailles Peace Conference. *(National Archives of the United States. Photograph by Captain Jackson of the US Army Signal Corps)*

Victor Emmanuel III, Giolitti, General Armando Diaz and Admiral Thaon de Revel. *(Author's collection)*

Victor Emmanuel III. *(SV-Bilderdienst)*

Giovanni Giolitti. *(Corbis/Bettman)*

Luigi Albertini. *(Gettyimages/Hulton Archive)*

Filippo Turati. *(Gettyimages/Hulton Archive)*

Luigi Sturzo. *(Gettyimages/Hulton Archive)*

Luigi Facta. *(Gettyimages/Hulton Archive)*

Italo Balbo. *(Corbis)*

Rome, November 1921. The fascist movement becomes the Partito Nazionale Fascista. *(Gettyimages/Hulton Archive)*

28 October 1922: the March on Rome. *(SV-Bilderdienst)*

The first marchers arrive in Rome. *(SV-Bilderdienst)*

Mussolini about to enter the Quirinale Palace and become Prime Minister, accompanied by Giacomo Acerbo. *(Gettyimages/Hulton Archive)*

Pope Pius XI. *(Gettyimages/Hulton Archive)*

Giacomo Matteotti. *(Gettyimages/Hulton Archive)*

Mussolini on the cover of *Time* magazine, July 1936. *(TBC/Gettyimages)*

# ONE

# The Conjuncture

On the morning of 30 October 1922 Benito Mussolini arrived in Rome, not on horseback, as he may have originally fantasised, but on the overnight wagon-lit from Milan, aware that King Victor Emmanuel III was to appoint him Prime Minister and entrust him with the formation of a coalition government.

While the future Duce was discussing strategy with his fellow travellers and meditating in his sleeping compartment, his supporters were converging towards the capital, some by car, others walking, but mostly by special trains, chartered with the help of the government. It was the so-called 'March on Rome' which had started on 28 October.

Ten years later, in a diary written with more hindsight than is usually the case, Italo Balbo, one of the more violent followers of the Duce, wrote that, from the beginning, fascism possessed the certitude that its destiny was the conquest of power through a violent insurrectionary act that would mark a caesura between old Italy and a new emerging country.[1]

It is often the case that those who proceed illegally try to find some legal reasons why they acted as they did. Sometimes revolutionaries insist on the legality of their actions, ignoring the short cuts they had to take. In Mussolini's case it was almost the reverse. He preferred to pretend that he had taken power by force, and that power had been given to him because he had already won it on the battlefield. But Mussolini's advent to power was – strictly speaking – quite legal. As the great liberal politician and former Prime Minister Giovanni Giolitti explained to his constituents on 16 March 1924, Mussolini had been appointed constitutionally, had sworn allegiance to the King and the constitution, and had presented his programme to Parliament, from which he had asked and obtained full powers.[2]

Yet the language used by the fascists at the time and in the following years depicted an uprising and celebrated revolutionary violence – one of several influences of the Bolshevik Revolution on the fascists. On 29 October 1922, Mussolini's newspaper, *Il Popolo d'Italia*, announced that 'The whole of central Italy, Tuscany, Umbria, Marche, and northern Latium is occupied by the Blackshirts,' conjuring up an image of armed occupation.[3] To a reporter of the Milan daily *Corriere della sera* Mussolini declared: 'Tell the truth. We have made a revolution unparalleled in the whole world ... We have made a revolution while public services continued to function, without stopping trade, and with employees remaining at their desks, workers in their factories, and peasants peacefully tilling their fields. It is a new style of revolution.'[4]

This image of turmoil and radical change was reinforced with the passing of time. The philosopher Giovanni Gentile, writing in 1924, claimed that the March had been a reaction 'against all the ideologies of the previous century: democracy, socialism, positivism, and rationalism; it was the vindication of idealist philosophy'.[5] The preface to a collection of Mussolini's main speeches published in 1928 enthused thus:

*In 1922 He marches on Rome. He is Italy on the move. The Revolution continues. After half a century of lethargy the nation creates its own regime. The State of the Italians arises. Their power emerges. Their virtues appear. Their empire is in the making. This great renaissance ... shall have His name. Throughout the world an Italian century is opening up: the century of Mussolini.*[6]

And when Mussolini addressed the Senate on 5 July 1924 he boasted that fascism obtained power by an 'unquestionably revolutionary act', by force of arms, marching on Rome '*armata manu*'.[7]

Twenty years later, in 1944, as the Duce faced defeat, more sober thoughts surfaced. Having escaped from the prison where he had been confined by the same monarch who had originally appointed him, Mussolini, now a pathetic Nazi puppet, recognised that fascism had not come to power by revolution. A true revolution, he wrote, would have required a fundamental change in the institutional framework of the state, but this had been left untouched by the events of October 1922: 'There was a monarchy before and there was a monarchy afterwards.'[8] He forgot to add that the King would not have turned against him had not the Grand Fascist Council forced him to resign. The great dictator had come to power legally, and was removed legally, not just by an old institution, the monarchy, but also by one, the Grand Fascist Council, which he had himself created.

Mussolini had given up on the 'revolution' well before his train approached Rome on that fateful late-October morning. The seductive appeal of power had made itself felt some time before, when he had become aware that he could get what he wanted more easily and speedily by compromising with the monarchy – one of the gestures that decisively propelled much of the political establishment into granting him full powers. Mussolini had realised there was no point in launching a major enterprise to grab power if power was his for the taking. His more naïve followers had not grasped this strategic point. As they marched under incessant rain they assumed they were making history, but the Duce arrived in Rome before them in his wagon-lit to be driven to the palace, where he declared himself to be His Majesty's 'loyal servant'.[9]

This was no act of renunciation. Mussolini claimed that he had wanted to avoid a civil war, but in reality he could not have taken power any other way. His 'army' of fascists was not strong enough. They could have been easily thwarted, and Mussolini himself could have been arrested without difficulty in Civitavecchia – halfway between Pisa and Rome – where the army had blocked the line so as to be able to prevent the *camice nere* (Blackshirts) converging on Rome if necessary. Mussolini could have been stopped at any time.

Rome was well defended. General Emanuele Pugliese was given the job of organising the defence of the capital; not an arduous task, since the columns of marching fascists were slow-moving. The army occupied public buildings, set up barbed wire, coordinated troop movements. Pugliese assured the Prime Minister, Luigi Facta, that he would have had no problems in restoring order. In Milan it was no better for the fascists. They had entered into the barracks of the Alpini only to face an irate colonel who told them that if they did not leave immediately they would be arrested. They left sheepishly.[10]

General Pugliese, loyal to the crown, had more than 10,000 troops under his command.[11] A further 28,000 troops controlled the roads to the capital. Pugliese ordered the railway lines to Rome to be cut fifty kilometres north of the city, and four hundred policemen would have been sufficient to bring the so-called March on Rome to a complete halt.[12] Thus, as clearly established by army documents, the army was in complete control of the 'marchers'.[13] Had it been instructed to stop the fascists, the march would have been halted.[14]

General Pugliese had leaflets distributed to officers and soldiers:

> *In these grave hours everyone must bear in mind the oath of loyalty to the Sacred Majesty the King and to the Statute, fundamental law of the state which safeguards the freedom and the independence of Italy. No one has ever dared march against Rome, mother of civilisation, and suffocate the idea of freedom she represents.*
>
> *You must defend Rome to the last drop of your blood and be worthy of her history.*
>
> *Major-General Emanuele Pugliese, commander of the Division.*[15]

The marchers were left free to camp outside Rome. They numbered 30,000 to 40,000. They were amateur soldiers playing at revolution, poorly armed (hunting rifles, old army guns, little ammunition) and no match for regular troops – as the more aware among the marchers realised only too well. A diary kept by a student noted that the marchers were frequently reassured that the army would never fire upon them.[16] In turn the fascists were reminded by their leaders that 'the Army is the supreme defender of the Nation', that 'it must not be involved in the struggle', that fascism had high esteem for the army, and that 'fascism does not march against the forces of public order'.[17] Indeed, troops were often used to provide food for the Blackshirts, pitifully soaked by the ceaseless rain.

Mussolini was perfectly aware of the weakness of his 'troops', which is why he took little interest in their military preparedness and efficacy, receiving only two messages from the marching fascists.[18] He had chosen to concentrate on the 'political' front, remaining aloof in Milan, almost as if to signal that he was not a postulant.

The tragicomic aspects of the March should not lead one to underestimate its political significance. The fascists occupied towns of the importance of Cremona, Pisa and Siena, and cut the telegraph and telephone wires connecting Pisa to Genoa and Florence. The link was quickly re-established, without diminishing the symbolic impact of the fascist advance. Cars and trucks were requisitioned and used to convey supporters towards Rome. Fascist activists were freed from the Bologna prison where they had been incarcerated.[19] Much of this encountered little opposition. The fascists had in fact been allowed to behave as a state within a state, parading uniformed supporters, talking openly of 'seizing' Rome, negotiating with local authorities and in some cases being welcomed by them. No left-wing force would have been allowed to behave like this. The legitimisation of the fascists could not have been more obvious.

So lacking in revolutionary secrecy was the preparation for the March that the chief conspirators, when they met a few weeks earlier in Bordighera on the Italian Riviera, were invited to lunch by Queen Margherita, the Queen Mother, whose villa was nearby and who openly sympathised with the fascists.[20]

It is difficult to stage a coup against an army, particularly in the absence of civil war, desertion, economic catastrophe or widespread civil disorder. The March on Rome was little more than an ill-coordinated demonstration aimed at increasing the pressures on the politicians in Rome. Mussolini – who had considerable strategic flair – realised that much was to be gained by remaining broadly inside the limits of legality while permitting regular forays outside it. But such a strategy could only work if wider liberal opinion had been prepared to tolerate the fascists' ambiguous attitude to legality.

The outgoing government of Luigi Facta had drafted a decree declaring a state of emergency which would have empowered the army to take drastic measures against the marchers. The King had been expected to sign it, but he re-fused. Instead he asked Mussolini, the leader of one of the smallest parties in Parliament, to form the next government.

When Mussolini arrived in Rome he was welcomed by a few hundred well-wishers. The reporter of the *Corriere della sera* – a paper that despised Mussolini but had come to regard him as an inevitable and necessary evil, indispensable to keep the socialists at bay – described the welcoming crowd as 'immense', the image enhanced by the description of women throwing flowers at the man of destiny.[21]

The 'march' had not been in vain. It was part of a symbolic theatre aimed at highlighting the exceptional circumstances surrounding the Duce's accession to power. Its purpose was not to conquer Rome but to provide the choreography, the necessary human material, for what was later glorified as *la Marcia su Roma*.

Thus at eleven on the morning of 31 October, Mussolini, a black shirt visible under his formal suit, as if to symbolise the two faces of fascism – respectability and barely concealed violence – turned up at the Quirinale Palace to receive his new appointment and submit the list of ministers who would serve in the new government. 'I beg Your Majesty's forgive-ness,' he said, 'if I am still wearing my black shirt, but I come from a battle which, fortunately, has left no casualties ... I am Your Majesty's loyal servant.'[22]

The new government was a genuine coalition. The fascists were far too weak to hog for themselves the lion's share of ministries. Apart from Mussolini – who kept the Foreign and Interior ministries – only three 'real' fascists obtained portfolios: Aldo Oviglio (Justice), Alberto De Stefani (Finance) and Giovanni Giuriati (in charge of 'recently liberated lands', i.e. those which had been under Austrian rule until the end of the Great War). There were also two members of the armed forces (General Armando Diaz at the War Ministry and Admiral Paolo Thaon di Revel at the Navy), one nationalist (Luigi Federzoni at the Colonies), one right-wing liberal (Giuseppe De Capitani at Agriculture), and two Catholics of the Partito popolare (Vincenzo Tangorra at the Treasury and Stefano Cavazzoni in charge of Labour and Social Security).

It looked almost like a 'normal' conservative government. Many of the 'true' fascists were disappointed, but the political élites were relieved. Mussolini's deferential behaviour towards the institutions seemed to confirm their belief that, while mouthing revolutionary rhetoric, he would be able to check the black-shirted hotheads surrounding him.

He had, after all, repeatedly given signs of moderation. And when, on 3 August 1921, he had negotiated a pact (the *patto di pacificazione*) with the socialists aimed at bringing violence on both sides under control, he had irritated the more militant *squadristi*, people such as Dino Grandi, Italo Balbo and Roberto Farinacci, who did not hesitate to accuse him of being excessively accommodating. Faced with what amounted to an internal revolt he had threatened to resign, thereby resolving the crisis.[23] The opposition he had faced showed that his control was not yet absolute, but the incident played into his hands because it confirmed that, unlike his acolytes, he was a shrewd politician able to play on several registers at once.

With their man now Prime Minister, the foot-soldiers of fascism went home triumphantly, confident that this was the first stage of a revolution that would sweep throughout Italy, transforming the country. Many of their comrades, however, were quickly seduced by the charms of the political establishment they had sought to destroy. They began to experience the pleasures of wielding power, of being feared and envied, and of basking in the respect of those they had hitherto viewed with awe.

The old élites, of course, despised Mussolini, the son of a blacksmith and a schoolmistress. They were alarmed by his plebeian tones and his rough and populist language, yet they recognised him as someone prepared to do the dirty work they themselves were not able or willing to do. Some intellectuals openly admired him, or were not prepared to criticise him. The distinguished historian Gioacchino Volpe praised Mussolini well before the March on Rome.[24] Benedetto Croce, the most revered philosopher in Italy, sent his good wishes to the new Prime Minister, while keeping his distance. Writing in 1944 of his contacts with Mussolini, Croce, in what were essentially self-justificatory notes, while barely able to disguise his pleasure at being esteemed by the Duce, explained that he had refrained from ever meeting him because they just did not belong to the same social circles: 'There were differences between us to do with differences of social milieu, family and culture; and I have always held the view that men get on together if they have had a similar education rather than if they share the same abstract ideas.'[25]

Mussolini too made sure that everyone knew he did not

belong to the same class as Croce. In 1931, wildly over-emphasising his antecedents as a 'man of the people', he wrote with some pride that he belonged to the class of those who shared a bedroom that doubled up as a kitchen, and whose evening meal was a simple vegetable soup.[26] It is true that life in his native Predappio, a small town near Forlì, was hard, but in reality his parents were not poor: they both worked – his father as a blacksmith, his mother as a teacher – and his father owned a bit of land which he rented out.[27] Mussolini was baptised in the local church and received a religious education. Yet his father was a socialist, who had named his son Benito after the Mexican revolutionary Benito Juárez, and given him the middle names Amilcare and Andrea after two Italian socialist leaders, Amilcare Cipriani and Andrea Costa.

Locally, Mussolini's parents were people of some import-ance, not quite the dispossessed peasants described in later hagiographies; yet compared to the politicians who had ruled Italy since its unification, Mussolini was certainly a 'man of the people'. The twenty-five Prime Ministers who preceded him may have been very different from each other, but they all belonged to Italy's élites. Some, such as Cavour, De Rudinì, Menabrea, Ricasoli, Sonnino and Lamarmora, were aristocrats; the majority were *grands bourgeois* – lawyers, academics, doctors and army officers. All had university degrees or had been to the military academy. Mussolini had left school at eighteen to be a primary school teacher. For a man of such humble origins to have become Prime Minister was a remarkable feat.

What are handicaps in some circumstances occasionally turn into advantages. During the First World War Mussolini had shared the lot of the ordinary soldier, the boredom as well as the fear. He could speak about life in the army with some authority, unlike the overwhelming majority of politicians. His war diary has the ring of truth. It avoided the absurd rhetoric of D'Annunzio (who had fought with considerable valour): 'After two months I am beginning to know my comrades ... Do they love war, these men? No. Do they hate it? No. They accept it as a duty that cannot be questioned. Those from the south have a song that goes like this: "And the war must be made, 'cos that's what the King wants." '[28]

A humble start in life may have prepared Mussolini to be more in tune with what ordinary people thought, and may have helped him to perform in the public sphere, embellishing his rhetoric with a language more vivid and more readily understandable than that deployed by his socially more polished rivals. But it would be a mistake to assume that rabble-rousing populism was a major factor in Mussolini's advent to power. Electorally speaking, fascism had not been a great success. The first election the fascists fought, that of 1919, turned out to be disastrous. It is true that the party, or rather the movement – since they refused to call themselves a party until 1921 – had just been founded, but so had the Catholic PPI (the Partito popolare italiano) – and this immediately won a major victory in the 1919 election. If anyone could be deemed to represent the 'new' Italy it was, in 1919, not Mussolini but the PPI, which was the *de facto* representative of the Catholic masses, or perhaps the Partito socialista italiano (PSI), still the main party of the urban workers and the new intelligentsia. The fascists did a little better in the election of May 1921, but only because they were part of Giolitti's *blocco nazionale*, along with liberals and right-wing nationalists. Giolitti had hoped to neutralise the fascists, and Mussolini had been ready to compromise to achieve parliamentary gains, though as soon as they were elected the fascist deputies sat at the far right of the Chamber, in opposition to Giolitti. Even so, they had not been able to muster more than thirty-five MPs out of 535. One cannot say that Mussolini had been swept to power by a wave of electoral support.

Votes, of course, are not everything, not even in a democracy. The real strength of the Fascist Party, as measured by the size of its membership, had been growing steadily throughout 1921. In March of that year the fascists numbered 80,000. By June the party had 204,000 members (62 per cent of them in the north). By May 1922 there were 322,000 members, and the Fascist Party had become the strongest in Italy.[29] The tipping point had been their inclusion in Giolitti's national bloc at the May election. This somewhat legitimised them in the eyes of many, for in the course of the electoral campaign they recruited substantially, and at a faster rate than ever before, more than doubling their numbers from March to reach 187,000 at the end of May 1921. This surge was over-whelmingly concentrated in some regions of the north and the centre, so that their activities appeared far more important and greater than if their support had been spread throughout the peninsula.[30]

The liberal establishment was scared of the fascists, but even more scared of the left and the trade unions. This explains why the violence of the *squadristi* remained unchecked; and the more unchecked it was, the more it grew. The fascists, while allowed to use violence, were never sufficiently strong to be able to topple the existing political order, yet not so weak as to be ineffectual. Besides, political violence was far more prevalent in the years following the First World War than it is now. When a left-wing revolt threatened the Weimar republic in 1919 even a social democrat such as Friedrich Ebert, then Chancellor, was prepared to use the Freikorps (a right-wing militia of veterans) to crush it, murdering in the process Rosa Luxemburg and Karl Liebknecht.

After the fascists came to power, in just over five years, at a speed dictated by events rather than by any carefully-worked-out strategic plan, what was still, technically, a constitutional government turned into a dictatorship. The existing system of proportional representation – the cause of parliamentary fragmentation – was abolished in 1923, and a new electoral system was devised aimed at guaranteeing an overwhelming majority to the victorious coalition. Then, by a combination of brutality and questionable legal proceedings, the opponents of fascism – socialists, communists, trade unionists, democratic liberals and the few conservatives who had repented of their early support for fascism – were eliminated, stripped of power, beaten in the streets by fascist squads, forced into exile, or jailed. New laws and new institutions finished off the old liberal state: a Special Tribunal with reliable judges armed with retroactive legislation cowed what was left of the opposition. Press restrictions muzzled the few remaining independent newspapers. New, pliable, fascist trade unions replaced the rebellious *sindicati* that had held, or so it was said, the country to ransom. A new law for the 'defence of the state' abolished all political parties. Even the Fascist Party lost its importance. The instrument of Mussolini's seizure of the state, the party had become irrelevant to the wielding of power. As the new social order emerged and the old one withered away, local fascist-led brutalities subsided and law and order were restored. Normality and routine were back on track. By the late 1920s the constitutional regime which existed when Mussolini had become Prime Minister was defunct. As the communist leader Palmiro Togliatti explained, the dictatorship was not established in 1922, but in the years between 1925 and 1930.[31]

Yet the social, educational and foreign policies Mussolini pursued in government in these first years in power were perfectly in continuity with those of its predecessors.

The resulting political system was one envisaged neither by the radical wing of fascism nor by the conservatives. The former thought they would get rid of the monarchy, of the old ruling classes, of clericalism, of a timorous bourgeoisie which had sold Italy to foreigners. The new fascist society, so they dreamed, would demarcate itself sharply from the pathetic liberal Italy which had achieved so little in its sixty years or so of existence. The March on Rome became their foundation myth. In truth it had been – as we have seen – little more than a paltry gathering of useful idiots, but in the telling and the retelling of it, the March was transformed into a revolutionary movement, the vanguard of patriotic Italians of all classes, concerned and dismayed by the corruption and decadence of the old liberal state. According to this narrative, they had rallied around a new leader, Mussolini, and his new party, the unsullied and uncorrupted Partito nazionale fascista, that had denounced the inability of the old governing classes to stand up to the Great Powers and to make Italy great again. In so doing these patriots had also definitively repulsed the menace of Bolshevism and socialism, and the strikes and subversion which had threatened hard-working citizens and led the country to the verge of the abyss. Responding to the call of destiny, the Duce had led thousands, perhaps tens of thousands – even, in some hyperbolic accounts, 300,000 – to Rome (the *Corriere della sera* estimated the number of demonstrators to be between 45,000 and 50,000[32]). With the country at his feet, Mussolini could have, as he declared later, transformed Parliament into a bivouac for his legions. Instead he demonstrated his love of country and his sense of responsibility and accepted the offer to become the King's Prime Minister.

Power, however, is seldom found in a single place, a handy central control room whose keys, once acquired, provide one with complete mastery. Even in a dictatorship, especially one in which the conventions are always changing, power is the result of a constant and extenuating negotiating process. The real losers are the outsiders. Isolated from the power structure, they do not see the compromises, the bargaining, the positioning, the back-stabbing, the fear of losing, the joy of winning, and the ephemeral nature of what appears permanent. From the outside a dictatorship looks like a formidable 'totalitarian' machine, in control and unassailable. When it crumbles (one thinks of Portugal in 1974–75, Spain in 1975–77, Iran in 1979, the Soviet Union in 1989–91, and South Africa in 1990–94), almost everyone is taken by surprise, except perhaps the more alert among those who led the old regime.

The key question to be addressed here is not how the dictatorship was consolidated, or why Mussolini succeeded in transforming a constitutional government into an undemocratic regime, or even why he was able to maintain himself in office so effectively for twenty years, and lost power only because he dragged his country into a devastating war. The key question is why Mussolini obtained office in the first place; that is, why, given the circumstances described, the leader of an electorally unpopular party, with no nationwide support and no control over the military, became Prime Minister.

Events developed in the way they did because of a unique conjuncture in which each participant, unlike a chess grandmaster, could not plan his next move in advance, with the knowledge that commonly agreed rules bind the players, that each must wait his turn, that only certain moves are allowed.

Like all political grand games, the Italian crisis of 1922 brought to the fore a multiplicity of actors, with no fixed rules, with no clear boundary between friend and foe, and no obvious resolution. Only later, when the dust had settled, could each side count its losses and its gains, curse the wrong moves made or congratulate itself on its mettle and luck.

Mussolini realised – partly from experience, partly by instinct – that in order to be accepted by all as the supreme leader, he had to please those who had not been entirely convinced by his performance so far, and inevitably to disappoint some of his supporters. The views of the country began to matter to him more than those of the party. By 1923 he was warning his supporters that 'The country can tolerate one Mussolini at most, not several dozen.'[33]

What were the circumstances which made reasonable and rational people hold the view that the country had become ungovernable, or at least that it could not be governed in the old way? In 1920 Lenin, who knew a thing or two about revolutions, explained to some of his excessively enthusiastic followers that one cannot make a revolution at will, but that it can only occur when two conditions are fulfilled: 'It is only when the "lower classes" *do not want to live in the old way* and the "upper classes" *cannot carry on in the old way* that the revolution can triumph. This truth can be expressed in other words: revolution is impossible without a nationwide crisis (affecting both the exploited and the exploiters).'[34]

In Italy in 1922, the first condition was no longer extant. The 'lower' classes, the workers and peasants to whom Lenin had successfully appealed in Russia in 1917 and in the immediately succeeding years, had been soundly defeated. The trade union unrest which had manifested itself in the 'red years' of 1918–20 had been quelled. As for the agricultural workers of central and northern Italy, they had been brutally put down by sheer fascist violence, violence which was often justified in terms of re-establishing order. The rural workers of the south had remained silent, barely aware of the momentous political game being played elsewhere. The second condition ('the "upper classes" cannot carry on in the old way') applied to a limited extent. The 'upper classes', if one can use this terminology to designate interlocking élites seldom able to present a monolithic face, realised that they could no longer go on in the old way, but they were not sure what the new way might be. They looked for an option whereby, to paraphrase Tancredi's famous remark in Tommaso de Lampedusa's novel *The Leopard*, 'Everything must change so that everything remains the same.' As the uncertainty of the élites grew, their unity, never their strongest card, faltered. Mussolini was one of several options they considered. They hoped that he would clear the ground from under the socialist and communist rabble, wipe out those trade unions before which they had trembled, and would then settle down, content with the trappings of power, cutting ribbons, strutting around, visiting schools, ennobling friends and relatives. Mussolini's assigned role was to cleanse the country of the red menace and then turn himself into a figurehead. The old establishment would rule in the shadows, as it had always done.

Mussolini's capture of power was seen by many of his contemporaries, at home and abroad, as the result of his exceptional qualities of leadership. He was the true 'man of destiny', the embodiment of *die Weltseele* (the World Spirit), to use Hegel's description of Napoleon when he saw the Emperor riding through the city of Jena on 13 October 1806, the eve of the battle.[35] Mussolini was one of the first modern leaders to achieve power in exceptional circumstances, outside the normal rules of politics. He had not been anointed by divine right, as under the *ancien régime*, nor – as in most democracies – gone through the legitimate process of succession as the leader of a major established political party. In the course of the twentieth century such men of destiny appeared with alarming regularity, and they continue to do so in the twenty-first. But Mussolini's predecessors were rare. Only in Latin America had dictators or *caudillos* come to the fore in the course of the nineteenth century, men like Juan Manuel de Rosas in Argentina, Antonio de Santa Anna in Mexico and Jose Antonio Páez in Venezuela; but they all owed their accession to their military positions. Like the first Napoleon and Oliver Cromwell, they were men on horseback. Louis Napoleon (who eventually crowned himself Napoleon III) did achieve office, like Mussolini, by exploiting a paralysis among the leading political forces, but unlike Mussolini he obtained power by winning a genuine presidential election – in 1848, with an overwhelming popular mandate, to the surprise of the political establishment. Only then did he proceed, on 2 December 1851, to stage a *coup d'état*. Unlike Mussolini he had no organised party to back him, nor did he need to compromise with an existing monarchy.

The nearest European predecessor of Mussolini was his contemporary Primo de Rivera, who in September 1923 was appointed dictator by the King of Spain, Alfonso XIII; but his dictatorship was short-lived. In Poland Józef Pilsudski was, like Mussolini, a former socialist leader, but unlike him he became a national hero in the course of the Soviet–Polish war of 1919–21, at the end of which he proclaimed an independent Polish republic and became the first head of state of the newly resurgent Poland. Having resigned this position in 1922 he returned to power in 1926, when the country, like Italy, was in the throes of parliamentary paralysis, and controlled the destiny of Poland until his death in 1935. Thus there were few if any historical precedents for Mussolini. This explains, at least in part, both his rapid rise and the difficulties even his contemporaries faced in trying to explain the phenomenon.

Mussolini was systematically underestimated by both allies and opponents. The initial reaction of the Italian Communist Party was muted. The Theses of Rome (March 1922) – the communists' founding document – do not mention fascism at all. Even an astute thinker like Antonio Gramsci, at the time of the seizure of power, dismissed the possibility that Mussolini might hold the fascist movement together, and like many commentators assumed that eventually it would split between an intransigent wing and a legalistic one. Writing in August 1921, Gramsci had suggested that by concentrating on Bologna instead of Milan, fascism was 'in fact freeing itself from elements like Mussolini – always uncertain, always hesitating as a result of their taste for intellectualist adventures and their irrepressible need for general ideologies – and becoming a homogeneous organisation supporting the agrarian bourgeoisie, without ideological weaknesses or uncertainties in action'.[36]

Even in 1924, when the construction of the regime was well under way, Gramsci's writings on Mussolini stressed the importance of the image of the dictator, rather than his policies:

*He was then, as today, the quintessential model of the Italian petty bourgeois: a rabid, ferocious mixture of all the detritus left on the national soil by the centuries of domination by foreigners and priests. He could not be the leader of the proletariat; he became the dictator of the*

> *bourgeoisie, which loves ferocious faces when it becomes*
> *Bourbon again, and which hoped to see the same terror in*
> *the working class which it itself had felt before those rolling*
> *eyes and that clenched fist raised in menace.*[37]

This is not to say that the image or the personality of the new leader was unimportant. While it is true that the seizure of power would not have taken place without a favourable conjuncture, personalities do matter. Mussolini was in the right place at the right time, but he was also the right man. Marx, who tended to overestimate impersonal forces in history at the expense of personalities, perceptively pointed out, in the second paragraph of his famous 1852 essay on Louis Bonaparte, that 'Men make their own history, but they do not make it as they please; they do not make it under self-selected circumstances, but under circumstances existing already, given and transmitted from the past.'

In this book I will follow this suggestion and seek to reconstruct the 'circumstances given and transmitted from the past' – the conjuncture – that enabled Mussolini to reach power. But no inevitability or determinism is assumed here. Matters could have gone differently. Circumstances made it possible for Mussolini to become Prime Minister of Italy, and further factors made possible the subsequent itinerary of the regime; but there is a world of difference between the possibility of an event and that event occurring.

Mussolini did not just appear as a new leader. He *was* a new, modern leader, one who possessed, to use a word now abused but then recently given a new meaning, 'charisma', a magnetic personality exuding power not because power had been foisted upon him by established political rules, but by virtue of some God-given, unfathomable qualities. Max Weber had defined charismatic authority – contrasting it with more usual forms of authority (traditional and legal-rational) – as a quality of 'an individual personality by virtue of which he is considered extraordinary and treated as endowed with supernatural, superhuman, or at least specifically exceptional powers or qualities'.[38]

Mussolini's merit was to have exploited to the full the cards that fate (history) had handed him. There was, of course, an element of luck – a concept seldom deployed by historians – for even the ablest of men cannot be aware of all the possibilities. In the end, one has a 'good' hunch and acts accordingly. After all, Mussolini's demise came about, at least in part, because of a 'bad' hunch: a miscalculation regarding the probable outcome of the Second World War. His initial (correct) instinct had been to keep out of it, just as his instinct almost twenty five years earlier had been to enter a war. Of course, in 1940 it was not unreasonable to assume that Hitler would win the war, and that it would be more advantageous to be in than out. But Nazism was defeated, dragging along with it into the maelstrom fascism and its man of destiny. Another dictator, Francisco Franco, had tried to join in Hitler's war, but, luckily for him, he was rebuffed by the Germans.[39] He thus ruled Spain until his dying days, allowing his apologists to celebrate his cunning in staying out of the war.

Italian fascism was wiped out by a world war, but it was also born out of war. Of all the factors that made fascism possible, the First World War was the most important. The war accelerated changes in Italian society, destabilised the country's parliamentary system and realigned its politics, thus contributing decisively to the conjuncture which enabled Mussolini to become Prime Minister in 1922. But it was far from being the sole factor. The changes brought about by the war made it difficult to return to the unstable system which had preceded it. Without the war, Italy may have had the opportunity to evolve otherwise and to follow a different, liberal, path towards modernity. Equally, it would have been possible to resolve the post-war crisis without creating the conditions for a fascist takeover of the state. As Paul Corner has argued, 'The identification of possible origins of fascism in the decades before 1922 is a very different matter from suggesting that these origins had a necessary and inevitable outcome in the March on Rome.'[40]

# TWO

# A Divisive War –
# a Lost Victory

The war that erupted in 1914 had been widely expected. In many countries it had even been welcomed. Imperialist rivalries, an arms race, the inexorable crumbling of the Ottoman Empire which opened a new political vacuum in the eastern Mediterranean, the growth of nationalism – particularly disruptive for the Austro-Hungarian Empire – the visible weakness of Russia (defeated by Japan in 1905), and a complex and unstable system of alliances all contributed to the outbreak of war after Gavrilo Princip's bullet pierced Archduke Franz Ferdinand's jugular vein at Sarajevo on 28 June 1914.

Seldom was the start of a war so popular – at least in cities; peasants remained indifferent, and women were probably more dubious than men.[1] It was widely held that the war would be short, and crowds in Paris, St Petersburg, Vienna and London cheered the beginning of the conflict. In Berlin crowds of between 2,000 and 10,000 people joined in patriotic demonstrations.[2] Outside Buckingham Palace there were people shouting 'We want war!'[3] The citizens of the belligerent countries accepted the onset of war, though perhaps not with the massive enthusiasm described in numerous recollections.[4] Recent scholarship notes that the evidence, at least in the

United Kingdom, of popular joy at the prospect of war 'is surprisingly weak'.[5] But, at least when war broke out, there was sufficient public enthusiasm to attract the notice of newspapers, and those who opposed it were subdued, divided and resigned.[6]

Jean-Jacques Becker's *1914: Comment les Français sont entrés dans la guerre*, still, after more than thirty years, the most thorough study of public opinion in a particular country at the start of the First World War, gives a complex picture of the divergent attitudes in France. These included sadness and resignation as well as patriotic enthusiasm, the latter being far less widespread than was commonly thought.[7] But some were thrilled with excitement. Adolf Hitler, writing in *Mein Kampf* in 1924, recalled his elation at the news: 'To me those hours seemed like a release from the painful feelings of my youth. Even today I am not ashamed to say that, overpowered by stormy enthusiasm, I fell down on my knees and thanked Heaven ... for granting me the good fortune of being permitted to live at this time.'[8] Hitler's enthusiasm may not be surprising, but more sober minds were also caught up in the ferment, including intellectuals of the calibre of Stefan Zweig and Max Weber.[9] Max Beckmann, the Expressionist painter, was exhilarated.[10] Rupert Brooke, in October 1914, wrote in his famous sonnet 'Peace': 'Now, God be thanked Who has matched us with His hour'. Rainer Maria Rilke celebrated the advent of the conflict in his *Five Cantos* in August 1914: '... the battle-God suddenly grasps us'. The Viennese playwright Hugo von Hofmannsthal, and Rudyard Kipling, turned into war propagandists. Thomas Mann declared: 'How could the artist, the soldier in the artist, not praise God for the collapse of a peaceful world with which he was fed up ...' Sigmund Freud too, at least initially, rejoiced in partisanship.[11]

And during the war the French philosopher of perception Henri Bergson travelled repeatedly to the USA to encourage Washington to enter the hostilities on the side of the Allies.

The popularity of the war can be gauged by the behaviour of the socialists. Before the eruption of the conflict they had repeatedly committed themselves to averting war by all possible means. However, on 3 August 1914 the parliamentary group of the German Social-Democratic Party stood unanimously behind their Emperor in defence of Germany. The French, Belgian and Austrian socialists also adopted a vigorous patriotic position. In Great Britain Labour MPs and the trade unions did the same (though some Labour leaders, such as Keir Hardie and Ramsay MacDonald, did not).

In spite of the war fever raging elsewhere, in Italy a wait-and-see attitude prevailed at first. This unwillingness to be plunged into the fighting was paralleled in other European states such as Holland, Spain and Sweden, which stayed out for the duration, and Romania, Greece and Portugal, which, like Italy, eventually joined in.

It would be wrong to assume that pacifism had much to do with Italy's reluctance to go to war. There were, at the time, two main strands of opinion which might be labelled 'pacifist': the Catholic and the socialist – but neither was committed to pacifism as a matter of principle. Catholics accepted the idea of just wars, but were hostile to the Italian state, whose foundation originated from a war of conquest against the Papacy. Socialists accepted the possibility of revolutionary violence, but regarded wars as the result of capitalist greed. There was also (and there still is) a common perception that Italians were ill-suited to wars and had a predisposition towards non-bellicose activities: Italians as *'brava gente'*, that is decent and good-hearted folk.[12] Such stereotypical attitudes occasionally had the imprimatur of major philosophers, such as Immanuel Kant, who remarked that Italians had put their genius 'in music, painting, sculpture and architecture'.[13] Italian intellectuals had often lamented the lack of warlike qualities in their fellow countrymen. Even Alessandro Manzoni, a Catholic novelist and playwright consecrated by Italian nationalism and revered by all, despaired at how centuries of foreign invasions had reinforced the supine attitude of Italians. In the first chorus of his 1822 tragedy *Adelchi* he described the Italians as 'a scattered people with no name' (*'un volgo disperso che nome non ha'*), uncertain, timorous and undecided, eternally waiting for a foreign invader to liberate them.

The reluctance to enter the war could more profitably be explained in terms of Italy's past rather than of national stereotypes. Italy's recent forays into imperial adventures had not turned out to be successful. In March 1896 at Adua in Ethiopia a large Italian expeditionary force of 17,700 men was annihilated by the armies of Emperor Menelik, the most scorching defeat of any European army in Africa. The dead and some of the prisoners were castrated in traditional Ethiopian custom. The disaster ended the political career of the then Prime Minister, Francesco Crispi.[14] The rush to colonies divided Italy far more than it divided Great Britain, Germany or France. In 1911–12 Italy declared war on Turkey and occupied Libya, Rhodes and the islands of the Dodecanese. This proved an easier enterprise than Ethiopia, but almost as controversial. The shame of Adua was redeemed, and Italy had become a colonial power, albeit a second-ranking one. Prime Minister Giovanni Giolitti, who had agreed to the war on Libya with some reluctance, had been supported by the liberal press, above all by Luigi Albertini's *Corriere della sera*, as well as by some Catholic organisations who saw the expedition as another crusade against the heathens. Libya, however, did little for Giolitti's prestige, while considerably enhancing the influence and power of Italian nationalists. Organisations such as Enrico Corradini's Associazione nazionalista italiana exploited the Libyan adventure, thereby assuming a much greater weight in national life than its numbers warranted, and made inroads into the civil service, the armed forces and intellectual life: 'By the conclusion of the war, the nationalist movement had burrowed its way into Turinese, Milanese, Venetian, Roman and Neapolitan centres of journalism.'[15]

Intellectuals played a role in legitimising a bellicose attitude. The futurists, who were against bourgeois conventions, including liberalism, parliamentarism and pacifism, glorified war and violence, regarding the artist, seen as a kind of Nietzschean superman, as in charge of his own destiny and showing the future to others.[16] Artists were supposed to abandon their ivory towers, approach the masses and lead them with deliberately shocking slogans worshipping war and violence – ideas soon annexed by the fascists. In the Futurist Manifesto, published in the *Figaro* in Paris on 20 February 1909, Marinetti, with the evident desire to *épater les bourgeois*, wrote that the futurists 'will glorify war – the only hygiene of the world – militarism, patriotism, the destructive gestures of libertarians, the beautiful ideas that kill, and contempt for woman'.[17] Marinetti also wrote enthusiastically about the Italian conquest of Libya in 1911 as the correspondent for the right-wing Paris newspaper *L'intransigeant*. Much of this provided a fertile intellectual ground for fascist ideas. But such a nationalist position was far from being the sole prerogative of futurists and modernists. Giosuè Carducci, Nobel Prize-winner (1906) and revered man of letters whose influence on Italian education and intellectual life cannot be overestimated, often glorified patriotic and warlike themes, evoked the greatness of ancient Rome and exhibited a 'visceral dislike of parliamentary institutions'.[18]

The Italian election of 1913, the first held under universal male suffrage, demonstrated, however, that the extreme nationalists had been kept in check: the liberals, though deeply divided, still had a majority, while the socialists improved their position considerably. This explains, at least in part, why the Prime Minister Antonio Salandra, a right-wing liberal, and the Foreign Minister Sidney Sonnino, also a man of the right, felt that the country was not strong enough to enter the war in 1914, and declared that it would remain neutral. Meanwhile they prepared the terrain for intervention.

Initially the majority of members of Parliament had declared themselves against the war, unlike their counterparts in the belligerent countries. Neither Giolitti's liberals, the dominant faction in Parliament, nor the socialists had been in a mood for entering the conflict. They argued that the Italian economy was much too weak, and too delicately balanced between the need to import raw materials and the need to export food (mainly to central Europe) in order to pay for imports. The labouring masses had only recently seen their conditions of life improve, and were not yet ready to feel part of a single nation. Besides, the war was seen as a struggle between two empires, the British (and/or the French) and the Germans, and there was no reason to shed Italian blood. The Church tried to maintain a degree of neutrality, since there were Catholics on both sides (in France, much of Austria-Hungary and southern Germany).

Interventionism, however, was not just supported by the military and the arms lobby, but also by a significant section of public opinion. It is unlikely that this was representative of the country as whole, since the rural masses were not in a position to express a choice, and few Italians participated in any pro-war demonstrations. The pro-war elements of the nation, however, were vociferous, and connected their interventionism to a widespread lack of confidence in the existing institutions of the state, above all in Parliament, widely seen as the repository of corrupt practices and dominated by untrustworthy politicians.

Salandra and Sonnino were in tune with such sentiments, since they negotiated Italy's entry into the war in the spring of 1915 without consulting Parliament. They thought the war would not last long, even though by then such views had less foundation than they appeared to have in 1914. It was widely held – and not only in Paris and London, but also in Rome – that one more push along the southern flank of the Central Powers and Germany would have to send troops to help its Austrian allies (outnumbered by the Italians), and would end up fighting on three fronts.[19]

Italian foreign policy had been auctioned off to the highest bidder. Germany and Austria had been prepared to concede Italy significant gains as long as she kept out of the war. The French and the British promised more: not just the Trentino with its Italian-speaking majority, but also the south Tyrol (Alto Adige) all the way to the alpine pass of the Brennero (Cisalpine Tyrol's geographical and natural frontier); Trieste, Venetia-Giulia, Dalmatia and various Adriatic islands (but not Fiume); recognition of Italian sovereignty over the Dodecanese islands; a part of the Turkish region of Adalia (now Antalya) in the event of a partition of Turkey in Asia; a share of any eventual war indemnity; and, 'in the event of France and Great Britain increasing their colonial territories in Africa at the expense of Germany, those two Powers agree in principle that Italy may claim some equitable compensation'. This, plus the promise of a loan of £50 million, sealed the deal. Article 16 of the Treaty of London, signed in April 1915, which sanctioned Italy's intervention, stated quite simply: 'The present arrangement shall be held secret.'[20] Italy entered the conflict on 24 May, declaring war on Austria. The hope that Italy's intervention on the southern flank of the Central Powers would lead to the quick collapse of Austria turned out to be unfounded.

In Great Britain, Germany, France, Belgium and Austria, the war united the population until the end of the conflict. Afterwards the inevitable recriminations, at least among the victors, remained relatively muted. Even in Germany, where the image of 'the stab in the back' was used by nationalists and later by the Nazis to berate social-democrats and pacifists, the war did not engender permanent divisions. Not so in Italy. Neutralists and interventionists existed in all parties, and remained bitterly at odds after the war. The weeks preceding Italy's entry into the war had been characterised by a climate on the verge of civil war. As participation in the conflict seemed increasingly inevitable, the neutralists virtually gave up the fight. There was a general strike against the war on 17–18 May. Then there was an eerie calm. The socialists adopted the slogan of *nè aderire nè sabotare* ('neither supporting the war nor sabotaging it'). The Catholics declared that they would be loyal to the state – though the Italian state had been created in the face of opposition from the Catholic Church.[21] As the troops marched off to war, it became difficult to preach an anti-war message. The pull of national unity was almost irresistible.

Later, as the war turned sour, anti-interventionists could declare that 'our boys' were dying in a useless conflict for the benefit of arms manufacturers, while interventionists

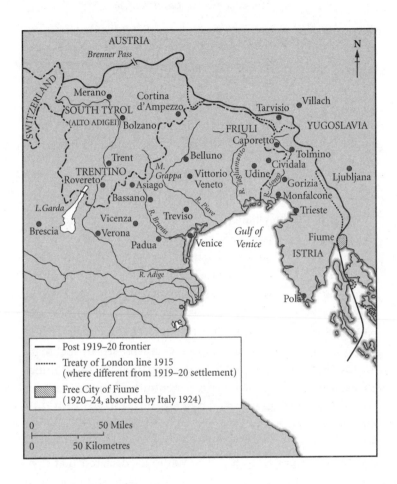

AUSTRIA

*Brenner Pass*

SWITZERLAND

Merano

SOUTH TYROL
(ALTO ADIGE)  Bolzano

Cortina
d'Ampezzo

Tarvisio

Villach

FRIULI
Caporetto

YUGOSLAVIA

Trent

Belluno

Tolmino

Cividala

M.
Grappa

Vittorio
Veneto

R. Tagliamento

Udine

Gorizia

Ljubljana

TRENTINO
Rovereto

Asiago

R. Isonzo

Monfalcone

Bassano

Trieste

L.Garda

R. Brenta

R. Piave

Treviso

Vicenza

Padua

Venice

*Gulf of
Venice*

Fiume

Brescia

Verona

ISTRIA

R. Adige

Pola

N

— Post 1919–20 frontier

······ Treaty of London line 1915
(where different from 1919–20 settlement)

▨ Free City of Fiume
(1920–24, absorbed by Italy 1924)

0        50 Miles

0        50 Kilometres

maintained that divisions on the home front demoralised the troops and encouraged the enemy. But when the war started, patriotic pressures were difficult to resist and opposition was muted. Few had the courage to appear disloyal. The formula *nè aderire nè sabotare* was an invitation to do nothing. Giolitti, who had opposed the war, announced, from his self-imposed quasi-retirement in his constituency in Piedmont, that he would support King and country. Some notable neutralists, such as the literary critic Cesare De Lollis, head of the anti-war 'Italia Nostra', volunteered for the front. Yet the events leading to the war confirm that Italy had entered it in a less exalted mood than other participants. War fever was confined to the more active part of the population: politicians, journalists, students, the urban middle classes. Various reports, including some from foreign diplomats, suggest that most Italians chose to remain silent, apathetic or indifferent. Those who supported the war found it easy to express their views. Those who did not found it preferable to remain silent. As for the apathetic many . . . How does one voice apathy? How does one measure it?

In 1914 Europeans were not used to expressing their opinions. There were, after all, hardly any channels through which to do so. Demonstrations needed to be called and organised by the politically active. Opinion polls were in their infancy. Writing letters to newspapers was confined to an élite. Confiding to one's elected representatives was a prerogative used by very few. Italians were less inclined than many other Europeans to participate. Not only was illiteracy very high, but so was electoral abstentionism, even when the suffrage increased from less than two million in 1909 to over five million in 1913. The division between neutralists and interventionists was confined to a relatively narrow section of the population. But this was the section that mattered: the opinion-formers, the intellectuals, the army officers, the students – above all those in the north.[22]

The interventionists were by no means all nationalistic right-wingers. They included some belonging to the left – the so-called 'democratic interventionists' such as Leonida Bissolati and Gaetano Salvemini – both of whom volunteered. Bissolati had been the first editor of the socialist paper *Avanti!* (1896–1904), then the leader of the reformist faction of the PSI. Expelled from the party in 1912, he founded, with Ivanoè Bonomi, the Partito socialista riformista. By 1916 he was in the government. Salvemini, who had left the Socialist Party in 1911 because it had not opposed the adventure in Libya energetically enough, had urged Italy's entry into the war on the side of the Entente. Like the other democratic interventionists he hoped that Italy would be able to complete the programme of the Risorgimento: the union of all Italians under a single flag, with the 'return' of the Trentino to Italy, as well as Trieste and all territories on the Dalmatia coast where the Italian language prevailed.

The position of democratic interventionism could be traced back to Mazzini and his desire to remove from the map of Europe a 'reactionary' empire such as that of Austria, which many felt would pave the way for a series of revolutions throughout central Europe. This seemed to justify joining the side in the conflict which included both the Tsarist and the Ottoman Empires, arguably more 'reactionary' than that of the Austrians.

Interventionists did not hesitate in advocating firm measures against the pacifists and the neutralists. In some cases democratic interventionists turned out to be even more authoritarian than right-wing nationalists. Thus Bissolati, in December 1916, thought that *Avanti!* should have been suspended, and complained that the reason Salandra, the Prime Minister, had not done so was because he thought the war would not last very long.[23]

The Church had hesitated to take sides in the conflict. Austria and Italy were both Catholic countries, but Italian Catholics had fewer qualms than Pope Benedict XV. Don Luigi Sturzo, the priest who would found the Partito popolare italiano (PPI) in 1919, was an interventionist himself. Military chaplains were in fact as war-loving as nationalist officers. Mussolini recollected in his diary that the most patriotic speech he had heard in sixteen months of war was in a church, on 31 December 1916, when he went to hear Mass.[24]

Thus the interventionist front was variegated. Its main pillar was constituted, of course, by the nationalist bloc, but alongside it was a motley crew of liberals and socialists of various hues. The interventionists had the advantage which in times of war always goes with those who wrap themselves in the national flag, since every defeat can be attributed to the demoralisation induced by the opponents of the war, while every victory is a vindication of one's position. Thus the débâcle suffered by the Italian armies at Caporetto in October 1917, essentially due to military causes, had spectacular political consequences, not only because it led to the replacement of General Luigi Cadorna as Chief of Staff and the resignation of Paolo Boselli as Prime Minister, but because it was used to excoriate the entire political establishment. The defeat, it was widely held, was due not just to Cadorna, but also to the defeatist attitude and the lack of patriotism of so many Italians (a view enhanced by the surrender of a large number of Italian troops at Caporetto), to the weakness and pusillanimity of those who had ruled Italy since unification – a judgement made not only by Cadorna, as was to be expected, but also by communists such as Antonio Gramsci and liberals such as Luigi Albertini, editor of the *Corriere della sera*.[25] Caporetto led to a renewed bout of febrile patriotism. By then this had also overtaken most socialist members of Parliament, including the veteran leader Filippo Turati, and leading trade unionists, even though the PSI refused to abandon, at least officially, the slogan of *nè aderire nè sabotare*. But there was also a corresponding surge of anti-war feeling. Economic difficulties compounded the opposition to the war, causing unrest in the countryside and in factories. Emergency measures and legislation permitting the banning by the military of religious processions and military-style parades were introduced. Legally binding agreements were introduced to achieve some social peace in the countryside.[26]

Mussolini's early decision to support the war added to the complexity of the pro-war bloc. At first he had been a neutralist, but he soon changed his mind and embraced interventionism on the not unfounded ground that the war would bring about a major social transformation in Italy. As a member of the 'left' of the Socialist Party, he had long been disdainful of the timid reformism of traditional socialists like Turati. When, in the pages of the socialist paper *Avanti!*, Mussolini declared himself a supporter of 'active neutrality', arguing that 'those who win will have a history, those who were absent will have none. If Italy is absent she will be the land of the dead, the land of the cowards,' he was immediately expelled from the PSI (29 November 1914). Mussolini's interventionism permitted him to break with the left of the Socialist Party and situated him in a political milieu far more profitable for his subsequent political career, even though at first his 'revolutionary interventionism' caused some anxieties in the Ministry of War and the high command of the armed forces.[27] He was still a man of the left, but as he was increasingly trusted by the nationalists, he became less and less 'revolutionary' and more and more nationalist. By January 1915 the motivations he gave for entering the war had become indistinguishable from those of the traditional nationalist right: 'We have to decide: either war or let's stop this farce about being a Great Power. Let's build casinos, hotels, brothels and let's get fat. A people can have even such ideals. Getting fat is the ideal of inferior zoological specimens.'[28]

The language used and the sentiments expressed tallied with the nationalist interventionist narrative which contrasted the new and young Italy, looking optimistically towards the future, with the old Italy – conservative, neutralist, dominated by parliamentary imbeciles whose vacuous debates paralysed the country. Mussolini's polemical attacks on the old establishment were conducted vigorously from the columns of his new, staunchly pro-war, newspaper, *Il Popolo d'Italia*. This made him popular among young veterans as well as modernists and avant-garde poets *à la* Marinetti.

Intellectuals such as Giovanni Papini and Giuseppe Prezzolini seized upon the occasion of the war to point out how 'sick' Italy had become under the existing political establishment. A revolution of ideas had become necessary, and it would have to be one which would not be afraid of using *teppisti* (thugs), for as Prezzolini wrote in 1914: 'One doesn't make revolutions either with scholars or with people who wear white gloves. A *teppista* counts for more than a university professor when one is trying to throw up a barricade or smash down the doors of a bank . . .'[29] Perhaps Prezzolini was already thinking of Mussolini.

The ambiguity in Mussolini's ideology, far from being a

handicap, turned to his advantage. The ideological realignment occurring in the country as a whole favoured those in search of novelties, and as we know, new ideas are far more flexible and formless than old ones. The Italy which was coming out of the war was quite different from the country which had entered it. The 'total' nature of the war was evident in all belligerent countries, but it hit Italy more than France, Germany or Great Britain. Not in the sense that more people died – casualties were proportionately higher in France – but because, before the war, there had been less of a national consciousness in Italy than in most of the other participants. The war helped shape it.

Southern peasants – hitherto barely aware they were Italians – had been drafted in large numbers, dressed in the same uniform beside students and workers from other parts of Italy, and led to fight under one flag in the north-easternmost corner of a country they hardly knew. It is difficult to ascertain the extent to which these recruits developed a strong sense of national consciousness, but they certainly developed a discipline they had never experienced before, and a marked feeling of community for those who fought and died alongside them. They also experienced violence and brutality. The number of Italian casualties in the Great War was extremely high: 650,000 dead and one million wounded. The number of casualties would have been even higher had not the high command acted far more prudently in 1918 (when the casualties fell to 143,000, against 520,000 in 1917). The victory of Vittorio Veneto in 1918 partly compensated for the losses suffered at Caporetto, and was exploited to the utmost by the Italian chiefs of staff. In reality, by then the morale of the Austrian troops had completely collapsed, and many were in open rebellion against their officers.[30]

War anger united disparate veterans around the vision of a different Italy, where those who had paid a high price would see their suffering recognised by a grateful motherland. Most, of course, saw the war as an inevitable evil over which they had little control. Used to obey and to be subservient, they accepted the war as one accepts a natural catastrophe. Giuseppe Capacci, a soldier in 1915–16, kept a diary written with uncommon literary skill (in civilian life he was a Tuscan sharecropper who had had only three years of schooling), in which there is hardly a word of hatred towards the enemy or a whiff of patriotism. The main theme is a resigned acceptance of his fate: 'We wanted to know where we would be taken,' he wrote, 'but it was useless: a soldier knows nothing until he has arrived. Some thought we were going to Albania, others to the Isonzo . . .'[31] In October 1916 he got lucky: he was wounded in the arm and taken to the relative safety of a military hospital, where the presence of nurses from the Red Cross reminded him of the comfort of feminine company, of mothers and sisters: 'Those who have not experienced the war do not know how pleasurable it is to return to a semblance of civilian life.'[32] The only social criticism he expressed was when, on the train taking him home, he was ejected from the second-class carriage to the third-class to make room for some *signori* (ladies and gentlemen), though he was visibly wounded: 'This is the love, the care that these gentlemen have for us soldiers; I shall say no more about this, though I could write much.'[33]

A collectivist spirit developed among many of these soldiers who until recently had been peasants. The war was a transforming experience. Removed from their normal situation, affections and interests, soldiers became absorbed in the task at hand. Their rural passivity turned quickly into humble devotion to their officers and love for their fellow soldiers.[34]

The war was seen as a test of comradeship, youth, discipline and courage. It was celebrated by those who had fought and survived it, and who had been, to some extent, brutalised by it and by the demonisation of the enemy.[35] Regardless of the reality of war camaraderie, about which we have only unreliable evidence constructed after the events, what united many veterans of the war was a common narrative. While the soldiers suffered, the 'others', the rich, the protected and those with well-placed friends and relations, had managed to avoid – or so it was thought – the pain and suffering of the war, and became richer. War enthusiasts and neutralists alike blamed the politicians who bickered in Rome, far from the trenches. The traditional anti-political attitude of many Italians grew in the trenches.

That the war had been a watershed is not in question, but so was the Second World War; yet, as George Mosse showed in an illuminating essay, the Second World War never generated a myth of shared experience and pooled memories in the way the First did.[36] The profusion of war memorials which dotted the countryside and small towns in France, Great Britain and Italy after 1918 was not replicated after 1945.

It was agreed, even at the time, that the conflict of 1914–18 had changed Italy completely. When it was over the then Prime Minister, Vittorio Emanuele Orlando, called it 'the greatest political and social revolution in our history'.[37] Salandra, who had taken the country into the war, admitted that it would be impossible to return to the spirit of the pre-war age.[38]

The new spirit was embodied in the returning soldiers. These veterans would provide the terrain for the proliferation of violent right-wing paramilitary associations from which the fascists recruited their most fervent supporters. Much of the symbolism of the far right was acquired during the war.

The black shirts they wore were inspired by the uniform of the élite crack troops – the Arditi – created in the summer of 1917 by General Luigi Capello. The hymn of the Arditi, *'Giovinezza'* (Youth), became the official anthem of the Fascist Party. The word *fascio* (bundle or bunch) itself had been somewhat in vogue well before Mussolini appropriated it. It originated during the Risorgimento, and was later used by left-wing protest movements of peasants and workers based mainly in western Sicily – the *fasci siciliani* crushed in the early 1890s by the Prime Minister Francesco Crispi. In October 1914 some left-wing trade unionists who wanted to join the war founded the Fascio rivoluzionario d'azione internazionalista. Then, in February 1917, a group of eighty pro-war MPs formed the Fascio nazionale di azione, which included not only conservatives but also socialist reformists such as Bissolati and liberal interventionists like Luigi Albertini, the editor of the *Corriere della sera*. Finally, in December 1917 a large group of nationalist MPs (over 150 deputies and ninety senators) including Salandra formed the Fascio parlamentare di difesa nazionale. They were hailed by Mussolini as 'the 152 fascist deputies'.[39]

Thus many of the elements of fascism – symbols, potential recruits, attitudes and ideological elements – were already extant when Mussolini was still barely known and had few followers. Had the fascists been more of a threat they might have been crushed by the ruling political establishment, but it was far more concerned with the danger represented by the left than with what was still an inchoate and ill-defined movement on the nationalist right.

A negotiated end to the war – as urged by the American President Woodrow Wilson in 1916 – would have favoured Giolitti and that section of the old liberal establishment which would have preferred to stay out of it. But the war ended only in 1918. Since Italy had been on the side of the victors, the interventionists appeared to have been vindicated. Before the war Italy was 'the least of the Great Powers', or perhaps not even a Great Power at all. Italian nationalism wallowed in a feeling of inferiority.

After the war, the situation was favourable for a complete realignment of the system of international relations in Europe. It is true that the real victors had been the United States – the new Great Power – without whose intervention the war might have gone on for longer, and on whose financial resources many in Europe relied for reviving their economies. It was equally true that, though weakened, Italy's main imperial rivals, France and Great Britain, had emerged with their colonial empires intact. But all the other Great Powers had been humiliated. From the point of view of Italian diplomacy, the situation for a major improvement in Italy's international prospects could not have been better. Its main enemy, the Austro-Hungarian Empire, had not only been defeated but was about to be dismembered. Germany had lost the war. Russia, having withdrawn from the war after the Revolution, was in the midst of civil war and, having become a pariah state, was faced with foreign intervention. The impending demise of the Ottoman Empire also offered rich colonial pickings to the victorious coalition. It was therefore perfectly rational for Italian nationalists – such as the Foreign Minister Sidney Sonnino – to assume that the higher status they had aspired to for so long could be achieved. After all, Italy had paid a high price in terms of lives lost.

Under the terms of the Treaty of London (articles 4 and 5), Italy was supposed to obtain the Trentino and Cisalpine Tyrol with its geographical and natural frontier, as well as Trieste. But the terms of the treaty also included Dalmatia, where the majority of the population was not Italian. The implementation of these terms would have encountered the bitter opposition of the southern Slavs: the new Yugoslav kingdom, quite legitimately, regarded Dalmatia as an integral part of itself. And Yugoslavia had a new and powerful supporter: the United States. The US had not been a party to the London Treaty and its President, Woodrow Wilson, had opened his famous Fourteen Points with a declaration of intent ('Open covenants openly arrived at') hostile to the kind of secret diplomacy epitomised by the treaty. Since the United States had become a major player in European diplomacy, and Great Britain and France were busy negotiating on their own behalf, Italian diplomats had few friends. Besides, they were divided. The more liberal members of the political establishment, realising that the cards were stacked against the complete fulfilment of Italy's war aims, began to seek a solution, but they constantly ran the risk of being denounced by those on the right. Italian politicians were in an objectively difficult situation. In order to extract more gains from the post-war settlement they would have to negotiate 'hard', soliciting the overt backing of public opinion, but in so doing they would fuel the war party, and if they were unable to obtain significant concessions, they would be seen to have failed.

Italy's negotiators (the team was led by the Prime Minister, Vittorio Emanuele Orlando) at Versailles had a narrow perspective, and concentrated almost exclusively on specific Italian demands. Their views were disregarded. Characteristically scathing of their endeavours was André Tardieu, who assisted the French Prime Minister Clemenceau: 'Signor Orlando spoke but little. Italy's interest in the Conference was far too much confined to the question of Fiume, and her share in the debates was too limited as a result. It resolved itself into a three-cornered conversation between Wilson, Clemenceau and Lloyd George.'[40] An influential Italian newspaper editor, Olindo Malagodi, lamented the lack of Italian interest in all general questions.[41] Even more damning was the view of the Italian delegates expressed in a letter by Lord Hardinge, Permanent Under-Secretary at the British Foreign Office:

> *Their incapacity and vanity are extraordinary ... They have been the most difficult element of the Conference, and much as I sympathise with Italy in every way, they are, in my opinion, the most odious colleagues and allies to have at a Conference. I am not pessimistic as to a compromise being arrived at, for there is a good deal of bluff in the Italian attitude and 'the beggars of Europe' are well known for their whining alternated by truculence.*[42]

Italy wanted to be given equal rights with the Great Powers, yet she was still far from behaving like a major European power with a Europe-wide view of international politics. To return empty-handed from the Paris negotiations would be to admit that Italy had been 'swindled' by the Allies, above all by the British and the French, who had managed to hold on to and even increase the size of their own empires. It would have meant recognising that perhaps the neutralists and the socialists had been right all along. Above all, it would have meant that all the war dead and wounded, and all the suffering in the trenches, had been for nothing.

What seemed at the time the most sensible course of action was to hold on to the real gains – above all to Trento, which was not in dispute – and to forget about pressing overtly ambitious claims not only over Dalmatia, but also over Fiume, which – though it had an Italian majority – had not been specifically mentioned in the Treaty of London. It is true that Fiume was Italian, but its surrounding territories were Slav. Had the principle of self-determination been adopted *in toto*, Fiume would have lacked a continuous land connection with the rest of Italy. The British and the French had been ready to accept the Italian compromise: Zara to Italy, Dalmatia to Yugoslavia, and the granting to Fiume of the status of 'free state'. But Woodrow Wilson was in no mood to make any concession to Italian nationalism – he understood little of Italian politics – and used the aid he was giving Italy as a means of exercising pressure during the Paris Treaty negotiations.

Wilson wanted Zara as well as Dalmatia to be part of a strong Yugoslavia, with Fiume a free city under the League of Nations. Wilson's dominance was linked to a simple fact: the USA had become the main economic power in the world, and Italy needed US credit in order to proceed with post-war reconstruction – the real priority of Francesco Saverio Nitti, who had succeeded Orlando as Prime Minister in June 1919. Wilson was in no doubt, as Nitti wrote in 1922 in his *Peaceless Europe*, that 'without the intervention of the United States of America the War could not have been won by the Entente. Although the admission may prove humiliating to the European point of view, it is a fact which cannot be attenuated or disguised.'[43]

The war had been of considerable benefit to many industrialists, since they could pay old debts and the huge war profits permitted new investments. This was particularly true of Ansaldo (a steel, shipbuilding and arms manufacturer), as well as FIAT and Pirelli. But once the war was over it was difficult for the state to continue to sustain the economy, and for Italian industry to find new markets abroad. The favourable balance-of-payments situation characteristic of the

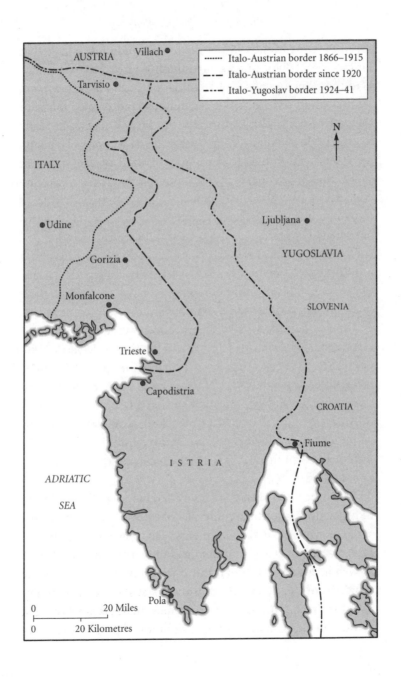

AUSTRIA

Villach ●

Tarvisio ●

ITALY

● Udine

Gorizia ●

Monfalcone
●

Trieste ●

Capodistria
●

ISTRIA

ADRIATIC

SEA

Pola
●

N

Ljubljana ●

YUGOSLAVIA

SLOVENIA

CROATIA

● Fiume

........ Italo-Austrian border 1866–1915
—·—· Italo-Austrian border since 1920
—··—·· Italo-Yugoslav border 1924–41

| 0 | | 20 Miles |
|---|---|---|
| 0 | | 20 Kilometres |

Giolittian era, which had helped promote rapid economic growth, was no longer extant in the post-war period.[44] There was, after the war, less foreign currency to buy much-needed raw materials and food, and the trade situation continued to deteriorate, particularly when the USA introduced protectionist legislation such as the Emergency Tariff Act (1921) and the Fordney McCumber Tariff Act (1922). The situation was further aggravated by the American block on Italian immigration, which caused a diminution of remittances from Italian emigrants abroad, since 84 per cent of all such remittances came from the USA.[45]

Keeping a large part of the army mobilised in order to continue controlling the Dalmatian coast made Italy even more dependent on US food aid. Vexed that Wilson seemed to disregard their country's interests, the Italian delegates Orlando and Sonnino abandoned the peace conference, only to return a few weeks later when they realised that their absence would make matters worse. The obsession with Fiume and Dalmatia was exacting a disproportionate diplomatic cost. Yet Italy had obtained considerable benefits from the war. In particular, she had succeeded in wresting from her traditional enemy, Austria, the territories of the Trentino, thus completing the task of the Risorgimento by achieving the full programme of *Italia 'irridenta'*.[46] A cleverer presentation of such achievements might have gone some way to placate the ever-dissatisfied longings of nationalist extremism. But Italy, as Adrian Lyttelton put it, had 'acquired the psychology of a defeated nation'.[47] Above all, the question of Fiume and Dalmatia was distracting attention from the economic priorities which should have been in the minds of decision-makers. These priorities had changed considerably as a result of the conflict.

During the war Italy, which had hitherto imported significant quantities of manufactured goods from Germany, had to supply them herself. Thus the net effect of the war was to increase the size of the manufacturing sector and of the Italian working class. In particular there was a huge expansion of arms manufacturing, and of the number of those working in the industry (ten times more in 1918 than in 1914). Much of this industrial growth, far from being a victory for market-led competitiveness, was due to the massive increase in state purchases. Italian industry was as state-dependent as ever. For the manufacturing sector this was an excellent situation: there was one buyer, the state, with a bottomless purse, since it was backed by lenders and taxpayers, and with the aim of purchasing everything it needed, at any price. Profiteering and corruption thus went hand in hand – and all under the banner of patriotism. Readjustment to a peace economy was in the hands of 'moderate' governments led by men who had been unenthusiastic about entering the war, like Vittorio Emanuele Orlando (Prime Minister between November 1918 and June 1919) and Francesco Saverio Nitti (June 1919 to June 1920). Remittances from emigrants did not recover quickly, and other countries besides the USA had put new barriers on immigration.

Nitti's grand plan was to tie Italy to America (and Britain) economically, thus improving the economy and bringing about prosperity.[48] He was also prepared to give up on some territorial ambitions, but neither the USA nor the UK was prepared to help Italy to the extent of offering American banks guarantees for lending money to the Italian Treasury.

The plan might have worked if the Italian government had been allowed to deal with the all-important economic issues, but the expectations raised by the war showed no sign of dampening. Veterans' associations grew strong and vociferous. By the autumn of 1919 the Associazione nazionale combattenti had 300,000 members.[49] The number of veterans had been further enhanced by the formidable growth of the officer corps, even at the highest levels. At the start of the war the Italian army had 142 generals. By the time it ended there were 1,246. Since they had fought for their country and survived the war, and their pay was satisfactory, they did not relish the prospect of forcible retirement. As Roberto Vivarelli points out, to placate these officers it would have been necessary to keep them on the payroll with desk jobs where they could do little harm, thus enormously increasing the military bureaucracy. Alternatively they could be kept on active duty, and the army in a state of readiness – as many industrialists wished, for obvious reasons – thus increasing further military and defence expenditure.[50] But the Prime Minister, Nitti, was proceeding in exactly the opposite direction: he wanted to relegate the war to the past, reduce military expenditure, re-establish the authority of Parliament, and uphold a new world order based on international consensus. So in 1919 there were still two parties in Italy: a 'war' party constantly seeking an 'enemy', whether external or internal; and a 'peace' party which, if it ever encountered an enemy, would try to appease it in all possible ways. The history of the subsequent years showed the constant growth of the war party, in various guises, unimpeded by an increasingly timid 'peace' party.

At the time the most visible exponent of the war party was not Mussolini but the poet Gabriele D'Annunzio, who, as he had claimed, did not wish 'to be a mere poet'.[51] He embodied in dramatic terms the fighting spirit of the war party. The liberal establishment was in awe of him. Aware of his popularity, it hesitated to turn against him. The press amplified his words and deeds. The poem '*La preghiera di Sernaglia*', in which he used the words 'mutilated victory' to describe the fear of the interventionists of being deprived of a full victory, was published on the front page of the liberal *Corriere della sera* on 24 October 1918. Its ringing words – '*Vittoria nostra non sarai mutilata. Nessuno/Può frangerti i ginocchi nè tarparti le penne*' (Victory of ours, you shall never be mutilated. No one will shatter your knees or clip your wings) – became part of the rhetoric of the war party.

D'Annunzio not only gave voice to the feelings of many veterans, but gave himself a new lease of life. By 1914 his main literary works were behind him and he was in danger of being forgotten. The war provided him with an opportunity to feel the thrill of action and battle, and to regain his fame. When it was over he experienced a sense of personal loss and anti-climax: 'When the guns fell silent, he regretted to be alive.'[52] Fiume offered him a cause, an opportunity to fulfil an old dream: the adventure of seizing a city, the excitement of blending politics and theatre.[53]

D'Annunzio's adventure in Fiume did not begin on the poet's own initiative. Local activists made known the 'plight' of the Italian residents of Fiume desirous of being reunited with the motherland. The battalion of Italian soldiers stationed in Fiume openly sympathised with them. On 12 September 1919 D'Annunzio started his 'expedition' to Fiume with no more than 120 veterans. As he entered the city he was cheered by Italian troops who were part of the Allied army of occupation. The following day the Italian general in charge of Fiume, Vittorio Pittaluga, relinquished power into the hands of the poet and left the city, followed by the Allied troops. D'Annunzio's expedition was the first serious attempt to impose an armed revision on the new post-war boundaries of Europe.

If D'Annunzio had wanted to provoke a government crisis, he failed. But if he had wanted to show that the government was weak, and prepared to tolerate acts of indiscipline and subversion, he succeeded completely. What kind of government would let someone – albeit a famous poet – lead a private army to occupy a contested territory under the temporary control of the Allied armed forces? Nitti was furious, but did not send the army to get rid of D'Annunzio, perhaps fearing that he would not be obeyed.[54] Without the complicity of the army, D'Annunzio would never have reached Fiume, just as three years later, had the army been ordered to stop him, Mussolini would not have reached Rome. Whatever the intentions of the army, Nitti was perfectly aware that popular opinion had considerable sympathy for D'Annunzio and his 'enterprise'. This included the *Corriere della sera*, though Nitti was equally aware that the two main parties, the socialists and the PPI, were completely opposed. Luckily for Nitti, D'Annunzio was politically incompetent, and his total intransigence – he remained immovable in his demand for the complete annexation of Fiume – did not help his cause. This played into Nitti's hands, but it also showed that D'Annunzio did not have the flair of Mussolini, who had a better sense of when to move forward and when to hold back, when to bend and when to be uncompromising.

In Fiume, some of the symbolism that would soon be borrowed by the fascists was first aired: the coarse insults for opponents, the songs, some of the bizarre exclamations such as the meaningless '*Eia, eia, alalà*' (a war cry allegedly used by the chorus in Greek tragedies), the macho posturing, the use of castor oil forced down their opponents' throats to silence dissent, the desire to shock the establishment borrowed from the futurists.

The Italian middle classes appeared to endorse such gestures enthusiastically, and D'Annunzio became a national hero. For over a year militarists and nationalists looked to Fiume as their City on the Hill. Even some socialists shared in such dreams, because D'Annunzio's Fiume Constitution – the so-called *Carta di Carnaro* – was a jumble of leftist and rightist slogans with little internal coherence. Drafted with the cooperation of Alceste de Ambris, an anarcho-syndicalist, it questioned private property and looked forward to a new 'corporate' state where class hostility would play no role. Much of what came to be known as fascist ideology found its antecedents in the unlikely adventure of the poet-soldier in a city few Italians had heard of.

D'Annunzio's theatrical escapade could be an example to be imitated, but it could not be the spark for a radical re-orientation of Italian politics. Its days were numbered. When Giolitti returned to power for the last time in June 1920 he began negotiations with the new kingdom of Yugoslavia, with a view to resolving the crisis over Fiume. The Treaty of Rapallo in November 1920 recognised the status of Fiume as a free city, and Yugoslavia's sovereignty over Zara. D'Annunzio's response was to occupy the Yugoslav islands of Arbe and Veglia, and to declare war on Italy. Giolitti's response was equally swift, and on Christmas Eve he sent troops to get rid of D'Annunzio. A few shells aimed at the municipal palace were all that was needed. It was only after Mussolini had taken over power and consolidated it that, in January 1924, he concluded a new treaty with Yugoslavia whereby Italian sovereignty over Fiume (occupied again by Italian troops in 1922) was recognised.

As for D'Annunzio, he continued to be celebrated by both liberals and fascists. Thus when he had a bad fall in his villa on

Lake Garda in August 1922, the *Corriere della sera* published – at some length and along with massive coverage of the event – cabled messages of good wishes from various personalities, from Giacomo Puccini to various ministers including the liberals Nitti and Giovanni Amendola. The War Minister sent this message: 'To the valiant fighter the regards and best wishes of all Italian soldiers.'[55] And, as if his illegal activities in Fiume were just an escapade, D'Annunzio was asked by the last pre-Mussolini government to speak on 4 November 1922 at a military parade in Rome to celebrate the end of the First World War.

# THREE

# The Parliamentary Crisis

While the mettle of the Italian state was being tested in such an undignified manner in 1919 and 1920, Mussolini was treading water. His various attempts to capitalise on Italy's 'mutilated' victory were overshadowed not only by D'Annunzio, but also by the wave of strikes which hit the north of the country, the electoral advances of the Socialist Party, and the formation and rapid growth of the new Catholic Partito popolare, which when it was founded in January 1919 had 100,000 members, and 255,000 in 1920.[1]

At the beginning of 1919 the only political instrument of any significance in Mussolini's hands was his newspaper, *Il Popolo d'Italia*. Its importance should not be minimised. It is true that the press was underdeveloped in Italy (compared to France, Great Britain, Germany and the USA), but the class of those interested in politics was rather narrow, and to have an organ of the media at one's service, in the absence of a popular press, was more important than having a political party. In fact Mussolini, in 1919, did not have a party. He had a 'movement', the Fasci di combattimento. Its programme was not obviously right-wing, since it included demands for the extension of the suffrage to women, lowering the voting age to eighteen, the abolition of the upper chamber (the Senate), vague corporatist demands for 'national councils' of representatives of the main sectors of industry, a minimum wage, an eight-hour day, workers' representation in the workplace, the nationalisation of the armaments industry, a tax on the wealthy, the confiscation of Church property, and a special tax on war profits.

Inspired by the prestige of Mussolini's *Il Popolo d'Italia*, a group of largely middle-class veterans, fewer than two hundred of them, met in Milan's Piazza San Sepolcro on 23 March 1919 to launch the new movement.[2] They were in search of novelty. Some were nationalists embittered by the war; others, such as Marinetti, were futurists keen to rescue Italy from the stultifying boredom of convention, and above all from the Pope. The meeting, later regarded by fascists as the true founding act of their movement, was barely remarked by the press.

Mussolini was quite conscious that such a small group could afford to be open to contradictory ideas. He told them: 'We can have the luxury to be aristocrats as well as democrats, reactionaries as well as revolutionaries, defending legality while committing illegalities according to the circumstances, the time, the place and the atmosphere within which we are forced to live and act.'[3]

Mussolini had not yet forgotten his socialist roots. In his Milan speech, which was published in *Il Popolo d'Italia* on 28 March 1919, he accused the Socialist Party of being 'reactionary' because its neutralism had favoured the 'reactionary' empires of Germany and Austria-Hungary.[4] Without the war, he added, there would have been no revolution in Russia, and the Tsar would still be safe on his throne: 'We are not the enemy of the working class,' he declared, indeed 'we are prepared to fight on their behalf'.[5] At this stage the fascists were not as distant as one might imagine from the *Partito socialista riformista* of Bissolati. Both were staunchly anti-Bolshevik, both had supported the war. The leading fascist in Cremona, Roberto Farinacci, future Secretary General of the Fascist Party and a diehard, had himself been a follower of Bissolati.[6] Where Bissolati and the fascists parted company was over the international situation, since Bissolati approved Woodrow Wilson's Fourteen Points and the US position on reshaping a new world. When he addressed a meeting at La Scala on 11 January 1919 his voice was drowned out by the heckling of fascist activists.[7] Bissolati and Mussolini also represented two different kinds of rhetoric, both present in the Socialist Party. One, espoused by Bissolati, treated political speech as a series of rational arguments to be developed in a didactic manner. Mussolini, like other socialists, followed D'Annunzio in his use of striking metaphors and similes.[8]

Mussolini's anti-parliamentarism originated in the Italian socialist tradition. In many European countries anti-parliamentarism was the prerogative of the aristocracy. Parliament, after all, was full of greedy bourgeois who had usurped the power of the nobility. In Italy, however, anti-parliamentarism was pervasive even on the left. The corruption (for which Giolitti was usually blamed) irked large sections of the subversive classes as well as the respectable middle classes. Traditional (right-wing) liberals too were hostile to Parliament, or, at least to a Parliament dominated by political parties. They much preferred amorphous groupings of individuals. Nationalists regarded Parliament as the place where the nation divided, and hence were ill-disposed towards it. Mussolini had acquired from his socialist father, Alessandro, a sense that Parliament was a rich men's club where the destinies of the masses were negotiated away – not an entirely unfair appraisal. He manifested his disdain for Parliament in a much-praised oratorical display at the socialist conference of Reggio Emilia in

July 1912. There he declared that parliamentary cretinism was more pronounced in Italy than anywhere else; that Parliament was of help only to the bourgeoisie; that universal suffrage was of little use; and that the debates of the socialist parliamentary group (dominated by the reformists) were pathetic and not worth discussing.[9]

Parliament had been considerably weakened by the war. Not only had Italian entry been decided without parliamentary approval, but the subsequent concentration of power in the hands of the executive was more pronounced in Italy than in the other belligerent countries. In the USA the President could declare war, but was not empowered to make laws or pass decrees; the French and British parliaments managed to retain a significant part of their powers even during the conflict. In Italy, however, the government acquired almost unlimited powers which it used on matters not directly connected to the war. Between 1915 and 1917 the Italian Chamber met 158 times, the French 371 and the British House of Commons 423. The war amounted to virtual political suicide on the part of the political élites, since it was in Parliament that their strength rested.[10]

None of this made much difference to the electoral fortunes of the fascists. The election of 1919, the first since 1913, saw the spectacular rise of the Socialist Party. With 32.3 per cent of the votes cast it became by far the largest political party in the country. In second place was the Partito popolare (PPI), with 20.5 per cent. For the first time the Liberals lost their parliamentary majority. Prime Minister Nitti spoke clearly to the Senate: 'The government has been much criticised for the political situation our country is facing. Well, honourable colleagues, we need to face the truth. There is a new situation in Italy. There are in the Chamber of Deputies one hundred

The battle of the plateau of Asiago, in north-eastern Italy, took place in May 1916. The Austrian offensive caused a large number of casualties on both sides. By June the Austrians had advanced by a only few miles. This was the only battle in which Mussolini took part.

The young Corporal Mussolini serving in the élite corps of the Bersaglieri in 1917.

Italian troops camping on Mount Pasubio, south of Trento. This was the main Italian strategic position from 1916 to the end of the war.

Antonio Salandra (1853–1931). He became Prime Minister in 1914 and secretly negotiated Italy's entry into the war in 1915. He resigned in 1916, but remained an influential representative of right-wing nationalists until the advent of Mussolini.

Headline of Mussolini's *Il Popolo d'Italia* welcoming Italy's declaration of war on Austria-Hungary: 'Italy has declared war on Austria. People, the Die is Cast: We Must Win!'

Headline of *Il Popolo d'Italia* announcing, prematurely, the eventual victory. The Italian offensive failed, and Italian troops suffered a major defeat at Caporetto.

Italian troops in retreat after the battle of Caporetto in October 1916. The defeat was so devastating that the term *Caporetto* entered the Italian language to mean a disaster. The battle lasted only a few days, but Italian losses were high: 11,000 dead, 19,000 wounded, and 300,000 soldiers captured.

Mussolini surrounded by his supporters as he launches the fascist movement in 1919.

Pope Benedict XV (1854–1922), who succeeded Pius X in 1914. His pontificate was dominated by momentous events: the First World War and the rise of fascism. He was a proponent of a negotiated peace.

Francesco Saverio Nitti was Prime Minister in 1919–20. He tried to concentrate on the task of post-war economic reconstruction, but was ineffectual in handling the Fiume crisis. After the advent of Mussolini he lived abroad in self-imposed exile.

Gabriele D'Annunzio (1863–1938). His political activities after the war prefigured fascism in rhetoric and symbolism. At the time he was Italy's best-known living poet.

Large crowds in Fiume celebrate their 'liberation' by D'Annunzio's legionnaires in 1919.

Mussolini and D'Annunzio in 1935. The smiles and laughter disguise D'Annunzio's hostility towards the man who (as he thought) usurped his rightful place in Italian history.

deputies from the Popular Party as well as slightly over 150 socialists. So two-tenths of the Chamber are under the control of a new force, the Partito popolare, and three-tenths under a party, the Socialist Party, which before had only one-tenth.'[11]

### Italian elections 1904–1919. Seats won

|            | 1904 | 1909 | 1913 | 1919 |
|------------|------|------|------|------|
| Liberals   | 409  | 364  | 307  | 211  |
| Catholics  | 3    | 17   | 28   | 100  |
| Socialists | 29   | 38   | 79   | 156  |
| Others     | 67   | 73   | 90   | 40   |

### Election of 16 November 1919

| Party | Percentage of vote | Seats |
|-------|--------------------|-------|
| Partito dei combattenti (Veterans) | 4.1 | 20 |
| Partito economico | 1.5 | 7 |
| Partito democratico sociale | 10.9 | 60 |
| Various liberali, democratici e radicali | 15.9 | 96 |
| Partito liberale | 8.6 | 41 |
| Partito popolare italiano | 20.5 | 100 |
| Partito repubblicano italiano | 2.1 | 9 |
| Partito radicale | 2.0 | 12 |
| Partito socialista riformista italiano | 1.5 | 6 |
| Partito socialista ufficiale | 32.3 | 156 |
| Partito socialista indipendente | 0.6 | 1 |
| **Total** | **100** | **508** |

The Parliament which emerged out of the 1919 election was strikingly different from the debating chamber of pre-war days:

304 out of its 508 MPs were elected for the first time.[12] The electoral law under which the 1913 election was fought limited the suffrage to all males over thirty regardless of literacy levels, and to males between twenty-one and thirty if literate. After the war this clause was abolished, partly because it was regarded as unfair that an illiterate of twenty-one could have been asked to die for his country, but not to vote. The second aspect of the new electoral legislation was that it introduced proportional representation – a 'revolutionary development', as Angelo Tasca, a founder of the Communist Party, remarked.[13]

Voters could now vote not only for a party, but also for particular candidates from that party's list. Strong, relatively disciplined parties like the PSI and even the PPI, with loyal electors, could direct them to vote for specific candidates; the Liberal Party, not a real party but rather a loose amalgam of local notables, could not. As a result the dominant faction within a party could ensure that its own deputies could control the whole of the parliamentary group. This further strengthened properly organised political parties, such as the PPI and the PSI.

The parties themselves had changed. The victorious Socialist Party was no longer dominated by Turati's reformists but by the so-called maximalists – the leftist faction which had been a strong force as early as 1912, but which had been further emboldened by the Russian Revolution. The maximalists did not yet dare to turn themselves – as urged by Lenin – into a Communist Party; they preferred to straddle a 'third way' between Turati and the various pro-communist groups, such as Gramsci's *Ordine nuovo* in Turin and Bordiga's in the south.

Nevertheless, the reformists still obtained greater support

from the electorate than their strength within the party warranted.[14] This was due to the well-established ties that linked the older generation of socialist leaders such as Camillo Prampolini and Filippo Turati to the electorate, and the moderation of the socialist electorate – always markedly less militant than the party activists.

The successes of the socialists and the Catholics produced parliamentary paralysis. There was little chance of the Catholics of the PPI and the socialists sinking their differences and joining forces in a government of national unity. There was also little chance of the socialists acting as a united reformist party. Elsewhere – in Britain and Sweden, for instance – socialists agreed to form governments in cooperation with liberals. In Germany the Social Democrats had found themselves in charge of the new Weimar Republic. In Italy, however, socialists were far too anti-clerical to join forces with the Catholics, and far too anti-capitalist to negotiate with the liberals. Even had they been amenable, it is unlikely that they would have found partners. Besides, the occupation of the factories had created a mood of militancy which strengthened the maximalists.

Thus post-1919 Italian governments were inevitably weak. They had, of course, been weak even before the war. Instability had long been a normal feature of the country's political system. What had changed, however, was the nature of this instability.

The weakness of the executive could be traced back to the 1848 Statute of Piedmont, its constitutional charter, which had been incorporated into the new Italian state after 1861. This granted the monarchy the power to appoint the government and the Prime Minister; while control over state finance remained in the hands of elected parliamentarians. Such an arrangement, of course, was a common feature of European parliamentary democracies, including Great Britain. But in Britain strong parties, the Liberals and the Conservatives, led disciplined majorities in the House of Commons which enabled them both to control the budget and to mandate the monarch to appoint the Prime Minister of their choosing. Prussia, and later Germany, did not have strong parties, but they did have a strong monarch. Parties were weak in France too, under the Third Republic, but at least in France there was a strong state, and the Radical Party (the French equivalent of the Italian Liberal Party) – thanks to its revolutionary rhetoric, was present in much of civil society, especially in the education system (besides, in France there were changes of government between centre left and centre right).[15]

Italy had neither strong parties nor a strong monarch. The country had not been united single-handedly by the action of a state – as had been the case in Germany, with Prussia. Such an initiative might have come from Piedmont, but the unification of Italy had been a complex affair in which other actors, such as Garibaldi, participated, often conditioning Piedmontese policy.

Since there were no disciplined parties in Parliament, Italian Prime Ministers had to gather together, after extenuating negotiations, the majorities required to pass legislation. Parliamentarians owed their primary loyalty to the electorate – a narrow segment of the population until 1912. Parliament was thus essentially an arena in which the representatives of Italy's landed and industrial interests squabbled over every single piece of legislation and financial measure. Opponents were, almost overnight, 'transformed' into supporters by direct or indirect bribery – hence the pejorative description of the system as *trasformismo*. The diffuse anti-parliamentarism noted above was a direct consequence of this state of affairs. Gaetano Mosca, in his influential *Sulla teorica dei governi e sul governo parlamentare* (1884), voiced a common complaint when he wrote that what predominated among members of Parliament was 'the most oppressive mediocrity'. They belonged to the older generation, that which had created the existing system: 'The Chamber of Deputies has become the partial ... representative of a part of the country while the majority of the new forces emerging in the country, those able to command, is excluded from it.'[16] Mosca proceeded, paradoxically and contradictorily, to urge a diminution in the powers of the Chamber of Deputies (the most democratic institution), in favour of King and Senate.[17] This remained a characteristic of anti-parliamentarism: instead of urging a reform which would bring in the so-called new forces, anti-democratic theorists such as Mosca urged an authoritarian solution.

A system of 'clientelism' developed, whereby politicians promised to provide their voters and supporters with jobs, protection and a steady inflow of public money. This kind of personal patronage made the development of centralised, modern political parties more difficult. Furthermore, since the vast majority of the population was excluded from the electoral, and hence the political, process, there was widespread resentment, culminating in repeated acts of civil violence which required a regular dose of repression. Towards strong local élites the executive was weak, towards the weak and the excluded it roared like a lion.

Italian parliamentarians were a relatively homogeneous group, particularly in the first fifteen years after Unification (1861–76), when the so-called 'historical right' (*la destra Fstorica*) was in power; most deputies of this dominant faction were noble landowners who had taken part in the Risorgimento.[18] Even the succeeding dominant faction, the 'historical left' (*la sinistra storica*), though less homogeneous, was still made up predominantly of aristocrats, officers, lawyers and some professionals such as doctors; there were few if any who were in trade or business, unlike in Germany or Great Britain.[19] Thus conciliation of parliamentary factions was fairly smooth – the practice of *trasformismo*. Originally the term had been used to describe the 1882 alliance between *la destra storica* and *la sinistra storica* – led, respectively, by Mario Minghetti and Agostino Depretis. Both were, in a way, part of the political archipelago generically known as 'the Liberal Party', though no such party actually existed (one was founded only in October 1922, just a few days before the March on Rome). There were hardly any marked ideological differences between them, though the 'left' was closer to the interests of the south, where it was electorally stronger. The principal political objective of those elected was to wrestle out of the government resources which they would then distribute to their supporters. Local loyalties always prevailed against national ones.

The system proved impervious to reform. In 1882, single-member constituencies were abandoned in favour of larger districts with several candidates, in the hope that localism would be attenuated. But this made little substantial difference, and after 1890 it was decided to return to single-member constituencies. This consolidated the relationship between electorate and elected representatives and, in the absence of British-style strong political parties, encouraged clientelism. *Trasformismo* adapted itself to all these changes, and much depended on the skills of the parliamentary leadership, its constant attention to local needs and its readiness to grant funds in exchange for favours, the principle of *do ut es* ('I give so that you may give').[20]

The kind of corrupt practices that inevitably ensued, as well as the resulting gerrymandering, were hardly a peculiarity of Italy. Personalised politics, whereby voters had a direct relationship with their representatives who would mediate with the central government, was a common feature of European political life, particularly in the south. In Greece, for instance, after the country had become independent in 1830, politics was characterised by strongly personalised links between patron-politician and client-voter, and by the exchange of *rousfeti* (political favours).[21] Politics was a necessary evil, a self-defence mechanism to be used to uphold a traditional way of life, not an instrument of emancipation.[22]

*Trasformismo* was openly defended in 1882 when the then Prime Minister, Agostino Depretis, in a famous speech at Stradella, discussing his agreement with the right led by Mario Minghetti (as adept as Depretis in the arcane arts of parliamentary compromise), asked rhetorically: 'If someone wants to join me, if someone wants to accept my modest programme, if he wants to transform himself and become a progressive, how could I turn him away?' The practice had started almost spontaneously when several candidates of the right had agreed with local lobbies that they would support the government.[23] To a large extent *trasformismo* could exist because of the high degree of homogeneity between 'left' and 'right'. Forces which could be defined as anti-system had either excluded themselves (such as Catholics, ordered by the Pope not to take part in Italian politics), or were irrelevant (such as republicans and socialists). They were, of course, a potential threat – one which added to the pressure on the Liberal Party not to divide itself into two antagonistic parties.[24] In any case, industrial interests were not yet strong enough to legislate against landed interests – as often happened in Great Britain; nor did the two classes, or the middle classes, organise themselves in strong political parties.

The system of *trasformismo* assumed that it was not possible to govern a country without some degree of centralisation. Parliament, by itself, could represent interests and positions, but only the executive could govern – as long as it had some kind of majority. What if such a majority did not exist, or at least did not exist in a stable way? People did not vote for a party and a programme of government, but for those they could trust to do the best for them once they were elected. The vote of confidence in a new government was not thought to be a necessary requirement until 1906. Before that it was assumed that the King had an absolute right to appoint the executive without Parliament approving; hence the need for constant negotiations. It required a certain uninhibited sense of politics, not one stuck in rigid formulae. It required opportunism and, particularly on the part of the Prime Minister, a remarkable political agility. Thus, even though the system was strongly parliamentarian, it also highlighted the importance of the leader.

What was particular about Italy (and other southern European states) was that there were no real political parties. In Great Britain the Prime Minister was powerful because he was the leader of the largest party; in Italy, only because he could distribute favours.[25]

Francesco Crispi explained it all during the electoral campaign of 1886, in one of his most important speeches, given in Palermo on 19 May. Since 1878, he said, Italy had had politicians but not political parties. The groupings were made up of individual deputies who, since they were elected individually, could change their minds according to the situation. In fact, changing sides was necessary for personal promotion. The whole point of having friends, in politics, was either to sell them out to a higher bidder, or to protect them if they could ensure regular reselection and re-election. Politicians were not promoting ideas, but only themselves (Crispi, of course, made it clear that he was different, and was loyal to principles more than to people).[26] Crispi's target was Depretis. His goal was to ensure that elections would be fought between competing government programmes:

> *The government allows the local population to be at the mercy of their parliamentary representative in exchange for his support. The appointments of the prefect, the chief of police and the local magistrate are made with the agreement of the parliamentary representative to enable him to maintain his local influence. One should witness the chaos reigning in Parliament whenever a solemn vote is about to take place. Government supporters run everywhere, including the corridors, looking for votes. Subsidies, honours, canals, bridges, roads – everything is promised; occasionally an act of justice long denied is granted for the price of a vote.*[27]

When Crispi became Prime Minister in July 1887 he sought to construct a strong state – taking Germany rather than France or Great Britain as a model – using a combination of colonial expansion, increased public spending, massive repression and anti-clericalism to construct some kind of mass support for the state. But even he was unable to put an end to the chronic instability of Italian governments, and the flimsy '*senso dello stato*' of Italians which was one of its much-lamented byproducts.

Silvio Spaventa, a politician of the so-called 'historical right' and the architect of the project for the nationalisation of the railways which led, in 1876, to the end of the supremacy of the right and the advent of Depretis, explained that in a normal country there should be only two parties represented in Parliament: one in favour of conserving and the other in favour of change, but that such a situation could not occur in Italy because 'the various parties which exist in our Chamber all originate from a single class, the bourgeoisie, the dominant class in our society. It is to be hoped that the expansion of the suffrage, by attracting to the government of the state new classes which have different ideas and objectives, will lead to a genuine difference among parties, and to the duality I have just mentioned.'[28] Though he warned too that if the bourgeoisie, 'which disposes of economic capital', were to forget that there is 'another class that has no other commodity except its labour, that becomes larger every day and that wants to improve its conditions of existence', it would not give rise to a 'modern form of government'.[29]

Everyone seemed to agree that the problem of Italian governance was really a problem of party representation. Even the advent of Crispi as Prime Minister had not destabilised the *trasformismo* system which Crispi himself had so often denounced. There was, on paper, a large liberal majority, but it was so unstable that the constant pattern of negotiation continued to be the hallmark of the system. The political struggle was not one between parties, but one within the great liberal majority.[30] As Spaventa had foreseen, transformism began to falter with the emergence of trade unions and political parties. To co-opt a class is not impossible, but it is far more expensive than to co-opt a politician. Class conciliation requires social legislation and welfare reforms, and these require a strong economy. High wages, another way in which the working classes can be co-opted into capitalism, were impossible in Italy, since low labour costs constituted one of the few comparative advantages enjoyed by Italian entrepreneurs. There remained repression. Sticks being cheaper than carrots, Crispi and Antonio Rudinì embraced repression, enhanced by a colonial policy aimed at creating an Italian empire for the benefit of all. But all this eventually failed too, as a major economic and agrarian crisis afflicted the country in 1888–94, and Italian colonial ambitions suffered a historic setback in Ethiopia in 1896. This paved the way for the rise of Giolitti, an enlightened bourgeois if ever there was one – too enlightened perhaps for the rather narrow-minded Italian bourgeoisie of the time. Giolitti had already been Prime Minister (May 1892 to December 1893), but the real beginning of his era started with the Giuseppe Zanardelli government of February 1901, when he became Interior Minister. Giolitti then proceeded to dominate Italian politics, often but not always as Prime Minister (1903–05, 1906–09, 1911–14) until the war.

Giolitti carried *trasformismo* onto a higher, 'modern' plane. Compromise remained the name of the game, as did co-optation, but this time it involved wider social groups. In his most famous parliamentary speech, on 4 February 1901, Giolitti mapped out what the new liberal policy should be on the question of the relation between capital and labour, in an attempt to push Italy's economic élites into the twentieth century. He lamented that the outgoing government still thought that all associations of workers were dangerous, even though this was no longer believed in other 'civilised countries' (meaning Great Britain and France, the main models of liberal Italy). The formation of trade unions was part of the progress of civilisations. Shown, in 1901, a cable sent to the Minister of Agriculture in which a Senator lamented that 'Today I, a

Senator of the Kingdom of Italy, had to use the plough myself because my workers, for centuries loyal to my family, are on strike with the assent of the government,' Giolitti replied: 'May I encourage you to continue to do so. You will thus be able to realise how fatiguing it must be and you will pay your workers better.'[31]

Giolitti also aimed at increasing the legitimacy of the state by widening the suffrage. This had been exceptionally narrow (compared to the countries Italian intellectuals liked to compare Italy with: France, Great Britain and Germany). When the country was united in 1861 only 418,000 people had the right to vote (1.9 per cent of the adult population). By 1882 there were two million (6.9 per cent). The right to vote was based either on education or on the payment of taxes. At one point in the 1870s deputies considered making the attainment of the fourth year of primary school the minimum for being able to vote, but only 14 per cent of municipalities had primary schools which offered a fourth year. Near-universal male suffrage (illiterates could vote only after reaching the age of thirty) was finally introduced in 1912, and first used in the general election of 1913. The electorate had grown to 8.4 million (23.2 per cent of the population), though abstentions remained high – even in 1919 only 56.6 per cent of those entitled to do so actually voted.[32]

Giolitti funded public works projects, created labour arbitration procedures, regulated children's and women's working hours, and established a network of inspectors to make sure labour legislation was enforced. Social reforms, he claimed, with considerable sagacity, were perfectly compatible with capitalism. The state should be impartial among conflicting interests; capitalists as well as workers should be equal before the law; each should have their own representation. The hostility of the trade unions towards the government was a reaction to the hostility successive governments had demonstrated towards them. But unions were the legitimate representatives of the working classes. Political institutions should not fear organised workers, but the disorganised crowd. If the workers were able to obtain salary increases thanks to their unions, there was no reason why the state should object, since the state should not act as the defender of the entrepreneurial classes. To do so would depress salaries below their economically 'fair' level, and would be an injustice. Countries where workers were well paid, Giolitti claimed, were in the vanguard of economic progress.[33] He denounced – not for the first time – the numerous indirect taxes (on bread and salt, for instance) which hit the poor far more than the rich, before adding: 'We are at the beginning of a new historical period. One must be blind not to see it. New popular strata are entering our political life; every day there are new problems, and new forces arise with which any government must deal. The confusions in today's parliamentary groups show that what divides us now is no longer what used to divide us.'[34]

As Interior Minister in 1901–03 Giolitti handled with great moderation the wave of strikes that gripped Italy. Trade unions were tolerated; troops were not automatically used to break private sector strikes, though he often used force to break public sector strikes.[35]

Giolitti's main worry was the advance of the Socialist Party. Created in 1892, in spite of the limited suffrage the Socialist Party already had fourteen seats in the Chamber in 1895, and was able to produce thirty newspapers – one daily had 50,000 readers. By 1897 it had 27,000 members and more than 10 per cent of the vote.[36] Though the party's strength was prevalently in the north (Piedmont and Lombardy) and the centre (particularly in the Emilia and Tuscany), it also had considerable support in Sicily and Puglia. And though it was a largely urban party (in 1913 one-third of those elected in towns with more than 100,000 inhabitants were socialists), it had numerous adherents among rural workers.[37]

Compared to France and Britain, though, Italy was still underdeveloped. In 1898 the average income was less than half that of France and one-third that of Great Britain.[38] The country was also plagued by considerable social conflicts. These culminated in the gunning down by General Bava Beccaris of workers demonstrating in Milan in 1898 against an increase in the price of bread: eighty people were killed. Yet these events seemed to signal the tocsin for the era of overt repression, for socialists emerged strengthened from such persecutions. The level of strikes remained high, and the number of those settled in favour of workers increased, but Giolitti – not always consistently – pursued his new liberal policies, insisting that the state should not meddle in these disputes.[39]

Socialism seemed to make headway even in the countryside. In 1897 there had been 24,000 rural workers on strike, organised mainly by socialist-led trade unions. In 1901 there were 222,000 agricultural workers on strike (out of a total of 450,000 strikers), mainly in Lombardy, followed by the Emilia, Venetia, Piedmont and Sicily.[40] These frightened the employers so much that significant concessions were made.[41]

Giolitti clearly had an overarching strategic goal: the construction of a modern, advanced capitalist state. To achieve this it was necessary to restrict social strife to an acceptable minimum, containing the threat from the left by co-opting not isolated MPs, as had been the case before, but the industrial working classes *as represented by their party*. To do so it was necessary to modify an electoral system which unduly penalised the socialists. As Turati complained, every socialist deputy represented nearly 11,000 voters, compared to a radical with 3,700, and a republican with 2,800.[42]

This co-optation required the introduction of universal male suffrage. This was achieved in 1912. The second plank of the strategy was a welfare state, as was being instituted in Germany, France and Great Britain (Giolitti's models). To pay for this Giolitti established a state monopoly on life insurance, through which he hoped to be able to fund a new system of workers' pensions without increasing taxes. Finally, it was also necessary to conciliate the Catholics (as a further counter-vailing force against the left).

Since Unification, the Pope had mandated Catholics to boycott the Italian state, forbidding them to take part in parliamentary elections, either as 'elector or elected'. Gradually, as the Church became aware of the socialist threat and as Catholics increasingly appeared to disregard this injunction, the ban was relaxed.[43] Pius X – who had pledged, after his election in 1903, to restore anti-modernist conservative theology (*Instaurare Omnia in Christo*: 'to restore all things to Christ') after the relatively liberal papacy of Leo XIII, agreed in 1905 to allow Catholics to organise politically. The Vatican was aware that the class structure of the Catholic world was changing. This world was no longer largely rural. New, expanding urban social groups, especially schoolteachers and white-collar workers, were increasingly under the influence of Catholicism.[44] The introduction of universal male suffrage in 1912 increased the value and impact of the Catholic vote, resulting in a secret 'pact' between the President of the main Catholic electoral organisation (the Unione elettorale cattolica), Vincenzo Ottorino Gentiloni (1865–1916) and Giolitti.

Catholic votes would go to candidates whose policies would not be incompatible with those of the Church. Ambitious liberal candidates rallied to express their devotion to such policies – another instance of *trasformismo*. So, even though only twenty-nine official Catholic candidates (i.e. those sponsored by the Unione elettorale cattolica) were successful, those deputies who were elected because they were supported by the Catholics were far more numerous – perhaps as many as 230.[45]

Giolitti emerged initially strengthened, since those who wanted Catholic support needed his help, but he also aroused the ire of nationalists and anti-clerical liberals. In the longer run he even lost the support of the Catholics, when they realised that it was far more profitable to organise themselves into a single, united Catholic Party (the PPI) rather than having to sell their votes to Giolitti's supporters.

Giolitti also failed in his long-term endeavour to entice the socialists to compromise with the capitalist state. The reformist Turati wing of the Socialist Party – triumphant at the 1908 party congress and more than willing to cooperate with Giolitti – could not countenance joining or systematically supporting the government, though they did so occasionally. When the ultra-reformist Bissolati agreed to discuss officially the formation of the new government after the election of 1911 he was promptly denounced by Turati, who feared losing the workers' support.

Finally, Giolitti was not able to secure the loyalty of entrepreneurs. Formally organised into an association in 1910, the Confederazione italiana dell'industria (led, until 1914, by a Frenchman, Louis Bonnefon Craponne), they did not have a cohesive ideology, nor were they particularly strong: the Confindustria, as it became known, initially had only 1,931 members, employing only 190,000 workers.[46] Some were for *laissez-faire*, others for protectionism, according to the interests of their enterprise. Their rhetoric was influenced by the writings of the young liberal economist Luigi Einaudi, whose prestige, thanks to his journalism, was remarkable, and in whose ultra-liberal economic message the industrialists found the kind of injunctions they liked to hear. In reality their liberalism amounted to a desire to decrease state intervention-ism when it was convenient for them, and a cordial detestation of 'bureaucrats', politicians and their cronies.[47] Furthermore, they objected to ceding the trade unions any power over the labour market, and did not want the state to arbitrate in matters of industrial relations.[48] This is why they feared the kind of state Giolitti was busy constructing. One could almost say that the industrialists became a political lobby and organised themselves as a response to Giolitti.

In spite of these apparently insurmountable problems – untrustworthy Catholics, militant socialists, unenlightened capitalists – Giolitti's strategy was the most likely to modernise Italy. It had the advantage of a kind of cold realism despised by 'a self-absorbed generation of intellectuals who sought poetry in politics'.[49] It accepted that the Italian bourgeoisie was weak, that political parties were not strong, that the executive was unstable, and that corruption was not necessarily incompatible with modernisation.

Control of members of Parliament had been the key to Giolitti's strategy. To achieve it, he did not hesitate to use the prefects, local bosses appointed by the government, to bring pressure on deputies, local mayors and councillors. As Salvemini, who had dubbed Giolitti *il ministro della malavita* (the minister of the underworld) in a famous article in *L'Avanti* in 1910, wrote later: 'This method, unscrupulously applied, sufficed to put at the service of the prefect most mayors in the constituency which was to be conquered or kept safe for a government candidate.'[50]

The Giolitti era was one of industrial development tempered by the economic crisis of 1907, which increased the powers of banks. The Italian economy became more open to international trade, with the conclusion of trade treaties with a number of countries including Switzerland, Germany, Austria and Russia. The consequence was a deficit in the balance of trade, partly compensated by remittances from emigrants.[51] There emerged a powerful 'industrial triangle' (Milan, Turin and Genoa) in which most Italian economic growth over the next eighty years would be concentrated.[52] Some, notably Douglas Forsyth, have argued that this expansion rested on uncertain foundations, soon to be weakened by the war, and that consequently the Giolitti system was even less realistic after the war than before it.[53] Business objected to the high taxes and the high public spending. Indeed, Mussolini's most successful economic policies in the early years were the reduction of public spending and tax reform.

The huge gaps between the poor and the rich, and between the north and the south, were exacerbated by protectionist tariffs (though their effects were not uniform). Social progress co-existed with social strife (the two are far from contradictory). As Italian liberal historiography had often claimed, the country appeared to proceed, in its own terms, towards the construction of a liberal state with social-democratic undertones.

For the Giolitti system to work, a number of conditions were required: moderate socialists, cooperative trade unions, Catholics willing to work with the system, economic development, social peace and keeping out of wars. Above all it was necessary that Parliament remained a place were political bargains could be struck between moderate forces. Until the First World War many of these conditions – not always concurrently – were in place. After the war they were not.

As we have seen, the election of 1919 – the first since 1913 – signalled the end of an era. The introduction of proportional representation reinforced well-organised parties and groups such as the socialists and the Catholics.[54] The new Chamber no longer provided a vast pool of liberals from which a Prime Minister could construct a majority.

But what was particularly worrying, from the Giolittian point of view, was that the strategy of enticing moderate socialists was no longer workable, since the majority of socialists supported the Soviet revolution, making the reformists of Filippo Turati even more unwilling to break with their party and join forces with Giolitti. At the Socialist Party congress held in Bologna in October 1919, shortly before the Italian election and a few months after the creation of the Communist International, the main clash had not been between moderates and maximalists but between various maximalist groups, while the communist faction had urged a boycott of elections (a position criticised by Lenin). The motion which won the day, and which mandated the party to join the new International, accepted the necessity of taking part in elections but upheld the eventual use of violence to destroy bourgeois power and establish the dictatorship of the proletariat. The reformists barely opposed this revolutionary platform, which seemed to be alarmingly divorced from the kind of demands (the eight-hour day, the reform of the sharecropping system, land reform, and protest against a substantial increase in food prices) which industrial and rural workers were putting forward. The socialists appeared stuck in a revolutionary rut which prevented practical action.[55]

The 1919 election – as has been mentioned – saw the victory of the socialists (156 deputies elected, against fifty-two in 1913) and the PPI (100 deputies, against twenty-nine pro-Catholics elected in 1913). The fascists obtained only a few thousand votes. The parliamentary factions (the historical 'right' and 'left') which had dominated the country since the Risorgimento had lost their hegemony. The paralysis of Parliament was the result of Liberal losses and the fact that Catholics and socialists were ideologically and socially too far apart to form a government. The Nitti government was forced to rely on the support of the PPI. It lasted only a few months.

Italy, as Lenin might have put it, could no longer be governed in the old way. Though there was no serious threat of revolution, from 1919 to the first half of 1920 Italian workers were in an almost constant state of unrest, culminating in the occupation of factories in the north. It was the most widespread era of social strife in the history of Italy.[56] Working-class organisations had emerged from the war remarkably strengthened. The socialist Confederazione generale del lavoro, which had only 249,000 members in 1918, numbered 2,150,000 by 1919. The Catholic CIL and the syndicalist UIL had another 1.25 million members (1921 figures), bringing to over 3.5 million the total number of unionised workers.[57] This was one of the highest levels of unionisation in Europe.

Workers' councils, seen by the communists as the harbinger of Italian soviets, took over the factories. Throughout May 1920 Turin, where the FIAT car-making plant was located, was at the centre of severe working-class agitation. The industrialists panicked, and Nitti's government sent 50,000 troops to quell a movement which included fewer than 200,000 workers in Turin and its province. According to the socialists, between April 1919 and April 1920, 145 demonstrators and strikers were killed, and 450 wounded, by the police and the army.[58]

The trade unions were barely able to contain the workers, but the socialists, notwithstanding their revolutionary rhetoric, realised that the situation was unfavourable, and that more time was needed to organise a proletarian armed force.[59]

Such social strife was part of a wider European unrest aimed at increasing the political influence of labour organisations. The labour movement was eventually defeated in different ways and with different results in Germany, Italy and France.[60] However, the alarm it had caused in liberal and entrepreneurial circles was considerable. The railway strikes of January 1920 were condemned by the *Corriere della sera* in far stronger language than it would ever use subsequently against fascism. The bourgeoisie, the paper claimed, had nothing more to concede, overlooking the gains it was making.[61]

In September 1920, some 400,000 engineering workers occupied their factories. Though the movement had spread to most of industrial Italy, its epicentre was in the industrial triangle of Turin, Milan and Genoa.[62] While both left and right saw this as a prelude to revolution, in all its main aspects the *occupazione delle fabbriche* was a trade union dispute, and even when the slogan of workers' control was aired, it meant mainly a system whereby a worker–management commission could be given accurate information about the economic standing of the firm, so as to enable the workers to evaluate the realism of their economic demands. Then the occupation was over. A compromise had been reached between the reformist trade unions and the industrialists. Giolitti, as ever, had been the arch-mediator.[63] This was a psychological defeat for the workers.[64] The dreams of revolution had been just forlorn hopes. There was no strategy, no intermediate goals, no clear indications of a way forward, only vague and vacuous slogans.[65]

It was a sign of the political crisis afflicting the country that the man appointed to resolve it had been, once again, Giovanni Giolitti. In June 1920 he was almost seventy-eight years old, still able to outsmart many of his successors such as Nitti, but unable fully to understand the new post-war Italy. Later, in 1924, he admitted that when he agreed to form the new government in 1920 he encountered difficulties he had never faced before.[66]

Giolitti attempted to ride the crisis, using the old techniques of *trasformismo*. Trusting in his proven ability to mediate between men, he thought he could do the same with modern, organised political parties. In a famous electoral speech in his constituency of Dronero on 12 October 1919 he defended the prerogatives of parliamentary powers, which, he claimed, urgently needed to be re-established after four years of un-controlled executive rule. He curried favour with the left yet again, by insisting that war profiteers had to be taxed, since 'labour is the only source of wealth', and 'the privileged classes of our society who have led humanity to disaster cannot rule the world any more'.[67] But the obstacles were numerous. The leader of the Catholic Party was Luigi Sturzo, a priest who had been able to build up the party in his native Sicily against the kind of forces which had long supported Giolitti. Sturzo knew his strength: since even the reformist socialists of Turati could not afford to join Giolitti (for the majority of the socialists were maximalists), any government was compelled to seek Catholic support. Giolitti's difficulties were further complicated by the fact that his own Liberals were more divided than ever: the war had created a deep gulf between those like Giolitti who had advocated neutrality, and those like Salandra who had urged entry. Managing the economy proved difficult. The problem was to stabilise it without disaffecting the new electorate. Nitti had not wanted to reduce social spending for fear of alienating the reformist wing of the socialists, thus attracting the hostility of conservatives and business interests. Giolitti reduced social spending by abolishing the subsidy on bread, thus angering the Catholics.[68]

Giolitti, working with the more moderate socialists, had persuaded them to settle the occupation of the factories in exchange for vague promises of consultation. The industrialists, though, had panicked. They had thought a revolution was about to break out. They were losing faith in Giolitti. He had become too much of an appeaser.[69] In reality Giolitti had understood the situation far better than they did. He was ready to make concessions, to institute a commission with equal representation from entrepreneurs and workers. His strategy was to avoid any provocation, knowing that the movement would soon peter out. He was right, but the industrialists had wanted to teach the workers a lesson, to humiliate the 'red scum'. This later contributed to the industrialists' *rapprochement* with Mussolini, even though the future Duce, taken aback by the breadth of the movement, had sought to mediate, but was then too unknown to be taken seriously. Not wishing, at this stage, to appear to side with the bosses, he did not join the chorus of disapproval from those who thought Giolitti should have crushed the workers.[70] The industrialists complained about Giolitti's 'workers' control' plan, as if it had been little more than a vague project aimed at ensuring that no one could claim outright victory and strengthening the reformist wing of the Socialist Party (whose workers' management schemes were, inevitably, regarded as class collaborationist). Yet in 1920 they still refrained from denouncing Giolitti too loudly, for fear of something worse.

By 1921 the danger from the left had completely evaporated.

With the power of hindsight, Luigi Einaudi described the occupation of the factories as a bizarre myth. There had been nothing to worry about. Yet in 1920 Einaudi had taken it seriously.[71] Once the threat from the workers had receded completely, the FIAT management became brave. In March 1922 it made workers redundant with hardly a protest from the unions, since many of those sacked had been communists and 'trouble-making' socialists. In fact the left as a whole, and not just the 'extremists', had been soundly defeated.

The wave of strikes had come and gone, the hopes of revolution been dashed, the unions humiliated, and the socialists were more divided than ever. Turati lamented – with some justification – the obtuse behaviour of the maximalists. The communist faction decided not to waste any more time with the Socialist Party. It split in January 1921 at the congress of Livorno, and founded the Communist Party of Italy.

# FOUR

# The Advance of Fascism

Until the second half of 1920, fascism had been marginal to the ongoing social and political crisis. Almost unmentioned in the press, barely regarded as a serious threat by the socialists, Mussolini's movement was in the doldrums. Anti-fascists – from liberals to communists – had failed to notice it. Antonio Gramsci did so in November 1920, when he described fascism as simply the violent face of capitalism, and the *squadristi* as those who do the dirty jobs that bourgeois society cannot do legally.[1] Togliatti, one of the founders of the Communist Party, first mentioned the fascist threat only in March 1921, when fascists destroyed the offices of the socialist paper *La Difesa* in Florence, months after they had started their rampage in Emilia and Tuscany.[2] Piero Gobetti, the young Turin liberal journalist who wrote weekly on cultural and political matters in *Energie nove* and other publications, discussed fascism for the first time only in May 1922, five months before the March on Rome.[3] This is not entirely surprising. Even in the middle of 1921, Mussolini himself, according to his biographer Renzo De Felice, 'was not really clear what fascism was about'.[4]

The intensity of the crisis was such that, as is often the case, all eyes were focused on the main protagonists – on Giolitti, on the socialists, on the Catholics. Mussolini did try to insert himself in the political game. During the occupation of the factories he offered his help to Bruno Buozzi, the leader of the FIOM, the engineering workers' union, and appealed to the workers over the heads of the socialists, against whom he directed his invective throughout 1920.[5]

At the same time he was mending his fences with Giolitti, ensuring the inclusion of some fascist candidates in the 'national bloc' electoral list for the local elections of 7 November 1920. Thus, thanks to Giolitti, some of Mussolini's supporters found themselves elected in Rome and others of the larger cities.

Yet the breakthrough for the fascists did not occur in the main urban centres, but in the smaller towns of the centre and in the countryside. For while working-class strife raged in all the industrial centres, the rural world too was in turmoil, with land occupations by agricultural workers throughout the north, and parts of central Italy and the south. In 1918 and 1919 the number of agricultural strikes had increased, reflecting the considerable changes that had occurred in the countryside in the war years.[6] The most remarkable of these was the increase in the number of peasant proprietors: during the war one million hectares of land were acquired by 500,000 first-time peasant owners.[7] Yet it would be mistaken to lump together under the category 'the rural world' all the diverse groups which constituted it – including landlords, small peasant landowners (*contadini*), sharecroppers (*mezzadri*), leaseholders (*affittuari*), day labourers (*braccianti*) and the 'rural bourgeoisie'.

While there were powerful landlords who owned vast areas of land, before the war most of Italy's half-million landlords had faced considerable difficulties as emigration (over 500,000 a year in the early 1900s) forced up the wages of agricultural workers. There was also a rural bourgeoisie. Its members were often classified as landlords, since they owned land. But they held onto it for family and traditional reasons, and needed to add to their income by owning a shop, practising a profession, such as the law, or by some precarious employment. Many of them detested the 'urban' classes – the rich as well as the workers, both of whom had improved their lot at the expense of those working on the land, or so it was believed.

The natural conservatism of landlords and rural bourgeois was reinforced by that of the class immediately below: the peasantry. Here Catholicism prevailed, along with a detestation of the state, of taxes, and above all of the socialists, seen as culpable of organising agricultural workers. During the war the peasants' dislike of central authority had escalated, for it was widely held that the conflict was in the interest of the rich and the towns (those who were exempted from military service were far more numerous among the industrial than the rural classes). State requisition of food was often regarded as unjust, but there were also compensations: pensions for war widows, subsidies to the families of those who had gone to fight, help with schooling for their children and other welfare provisions. The underemployment endemic in small farms often meant that when a father or son was conscripted, those remaining on the family farm were able, by working a little harder, to maintain the same level of production without hiring anyone. There were also often war-related jobs in nearby industries.[8] Those cultivating products such as timber did relatively better out of the war than those growing cereals.[9] War rationing of food affected those living in cities far more than those in the countryside, who had plenty to eat.[10]

'Below' the peasants were the *mezzadri*, or sharecroppers. These were peasant-tenants who worked the land owned by a landlord, occasionally employing day labourers. The landlord could evict the sharecropper, and owned not only the land but the peasant cottage, the animals and some of the tools. Landlords and sharecroppers shared expenses and profits according to a contract which could also require the sharecropper to perform services at various times of the year. The conditions of life of the sharecroppers had deteriorated in the years leading up to the war as farming became more commercialised, thus decreasing their share.[11] During the war, however, landless labourers suffered far more than the sharecroppers, because their wages failed to keep up with prices. Sharecroppers, on the other hand, benefited from inflation, since debts contracted earlier (to pay for tools and seeds) became depreciated.[12] Thus many sharecroppers were better off at the end of the war than at the beginning. They also realised that there was a real possibility that they would be able to become the owners of the land on which they had been working, particularly those who had saved money thanks to the constant increase in the price of foodstuff.

The slogan 'land to those who till it' was found to be very appealing, and almost all political forces – even some conservatives – invoked it in some form or other. Various schemes for land reform were advanced, including the state purchase of land which would then be given in concession to single peasant families or a group of them to cultivate. The expropriation of fallow or uncultivated land, land abandoned by its owners, and its distribution to the peasantry had considerable support in Parliament. Such debates awakened peasant hopes, though they regarded all these projects as inferior to their wish to have their own piece of land.[13] Here the Catholics of the PPI had emerged as the most resolute upholder of the demand 'land to those who till it'.

Most socialists, however, thought that the most efficient solution was to group together vast tracts of land and give them to cooperatives of peasants to cultivate. The long-term goal of the socialists was 'the socialisation of land' – a slogan which had surfaced during the war and the Russian Revolution (while the Bolsheviks, ironically, had appropriated the opposite slogan of 'land to the peasants'). In these circumstances the hostility of the land-owning classes (landlords, small peasant proprietors and sharecroppers with a prospect of owning their land) towards the socialists could not but grow. The socialists, furthermore, were the main force organising agricultural workers in a trade union (the Federazione lavoratori della terra) and the inspirer of the Socialist Leagues, which supported the wave of strikes by day labourers in 1919–20. These strikes called for an eight-hour day and substantial wage increases, as well as the nationalisation of land. Even moderate socialists such as Claudio Treves denounced any demand to increase the number of small proprietors on the land as a Catholic trick aimed at erecting an obstacle to the spread of socialist ideas.[14] The collectivist approach advocated by the socialists might have worked, politically speaking, in the Po Valley, where the majority of workers on the land were landless labourers, but not in Tuscany, where sharecroppers were particularly numerous (which is why in much of Tuscany eventually even the socialists called for 'land to the peasants').

The anxiety of the land-owning classes mounted further after the local elections of autumn 1920, when the socialists made remarkable gains in many small towns in the Emilia-Romagna and Tuscany, while the Catholic *Popolari* seized control of municipalities in many parts of Piedmont, Lombardy and Venetia. Particularly significant was the triumph of the socialists in Bologna, where the PSI obtained 63 per cent of the vote. Seven of the local MPs were now socialists, the eighth was a PPI. The old Liberal Party, upholder of the interests of the local propertied classes, had been routed.[15] Those now in control could assign public sector jobs and contracts to their own cooperatives. Socialist local authorities increased property taxes while socialist Chambers of Labour acquired greater control over the hiring and firing of agricultural workers, and obtained higher wages and shorter hours.[16] The land-owning classes and the local notables who controlled local politics felt bitter. Their entire system of power seemed to be crumbling before the red menace.

Since the landlords thought that the government was not doing much to help them in their struggle against the Leagues, they recruited their own squads, often from among local fascists, who were particularly anti-socialist, and who thus extended their influence in the small towns of the Po Valley, Tuscany and Umbria. It was difficult for farmers to resist the lure of fascist violence. Afraid of reprisals from the left, they were reluctant to engage blackleg labour. They expected the state to intervene, but the government, weak as ever, was afraid to risk confrontation with the left.[17] A report in the main Bologna daily cited a landlord lamenting having been informed by the authorities that 'the government was in no way able to guarantee us the respect of property or persons'.[18] Unsurprisingly, landlords turned increasingly towards the fascists. The violence exercised by the fascists was thus not mindless.[19] It had precise targets, and a strong base of support. While the right was uniting, the left was dividing between reformists, maximalists and communists. Moreover, the violence used by the fascists was effective in frightening the electorate. In Reggio Emilia, a socialist stronghold where they had obtained 50 per cent of the vote in 1919, they obtained only 5.9 per cent in 1921.[20]

A climate of lawlessness developed. The fascists' brutal methods were welcomed even by sections of the liberal press, which assumed that once their task had been accomplished the *fascisti* could be controlled. The activities of these rural *fascisti* did not encounter any obstacle from the authorities, least of all from the armed forces, who often sympathised with them. The police often did not turn up at the scene of fascist crimes, or arrived late, and did not identify the offenders. They were partial towards the fascists, and against the socialists.[21] In Brescia, Ferrara and elsewhere, policemen and *carabinieri* acting on their own initiative joined in strike-breaking.[22] The younger officers had developed a particularly strong hostility towards the socialists, who were accused of pacifism and of being the ones responsible for the 'mutilated victory'.

The anger of the landlords was further exacerbated by the poor quality of the harvest in 1920, which further reduced their profits.[23] It is thus not surprising that they should have sought the support of the fascists, who had done reasonably well in the local elections and whose propaganda claimed that they would defend the rights of citizens during strikes – in other words, protect blackleg labour from socialist attacks.[24] Landowners and the professional and commercial bourgeoisie of Italy's provinces rallied round the kind of appeal epitomised by a leading article in a Ferrara newspaper in early November 1920: 'New, young, courageous forces are needed. Fortunately the recent electoral struggle has shown us these fresh forces: the fascists ... Only they have the right to make claims on the future of Italy; only they, who love youth and force, can arrest the wave of madness which is breaking over Italy.'[25] This was the context for the alliance between fascist *squadristi* and landlords, with the former financed by the latter. By the end of November 1920 the alliance between landlords and fascism became explicit.[26] Those who could have opposed them, the Catholics and the socialists, were hopelessly divided: 'The rural labour movement collapsed into a feud between its two constituent parts.'[27] It was, anyway, too late for the constitution of a legitimate and properly functioning agrarian party – the fascists had proved to be the more attractive proposition.[28]

At a speed no one could have forecast, the landowners were offered the prospect of seeing hated rural trade unionism liquidated by a movement, that of Mussolini, which appeared to be better able to represent their long-term aspirations: the defence of private property, a nationalist foreign policy, and public works to help the rural economy. Giolitti and Nitti were paying the price for concentrating excessively on the needs of the industrial sector. The alienated landowners of the provincial north and centre were striking back, with the squads of fascism as their main weapon.[29] This was true even in places like Tuscany, where there was no recent history of violent clashes between peasants and landlords, as had been the case elsewhere in the peninsula. Now it became one of the centres of fascist violence in the countryside.[30]

As we have seen, fascism was born in Milan in Piazza Sepolcro in March 1919, when Mussolini had announced the formation of his movement. But no one had noticed it. By the end of 1920 the situation had changed dramatically. The new launchpad of fascism was constituted by the 'red' fortresses of Ferrara and Bologna, where the anger of the bourgeoisie, which regarded itself as an oppressed minority, had swelled in the years of the war and in its aftermath. From there fascism embarked in an offensive towards the main socialist stronghold in the countryside, that is in the rest of the Po Valley, in

Tuscany, Umbria, and even in the southern region of the Apulia. Success breeds success, and many flocked to join the ranks of fascism in the first months of 1921.[31] There was sympathy for the fascists in many quarters. In a circular of September 1920 the armed forces' chiefs of staff noted that the fascists were 'living forces to be used, eventually, against subversive and anti-national forces'.[32] To Gramsci this constituted a change of direction by Italy's petty bourgeoisie. Once it was 'enslaved to parliamentary power'; now it had become anti-parliamentarian, 'aping the working class and coming out onto the streets'.[33]

Mussolini, against the evidence, later denied that fascism ever sought to represent the interests of landlords, while insisting that small landlords, sharecroppers and tenant farmers, who all detested socialism, had nothing to fear from fascism.[34]

Before descending upon the countryside, fascism had tested its violent mettle six months earlier in Trieste, where on 13 July 1920 nationalists and armed fascists attacked the offices of the Slovenian minority in the Hotel Balkan. In September, Mussolini was greeted as a conquering hero by the whole city – Trieste being one of the few cities in Italy where the fascists enjoyed widespread support among the working class.[35] With the help of the authorities, Slovene clubs and newspapers were systematically destroyed. The enemy then was Slav nationalism, not socialism.[36] But the fascists soon turned against the socialists, destroying on 14–15 October 1920 the offices of the socialist daily *Il lavoratore di Trieste* and the Chamber of Labour in Fiume. Then the violence spread south to the Emilia: on 21 November it was the turn of the Palazzo d'Accursio in Bologna, where the fascists opened fire on a gathering in the piazza called to celebrate the election victory of the socialists.[37] There were nine dead and a hundred wounded. In January

1921, again in Bologna, the Blackshirts burned down the Chamber of Labour. The local élites cheered. It was their revenge for the times, even before the war, when the Socialist Party appeared to them as 'a state within the state with its own special laws and . . . executive organs'.[38] A special parliamentary commission concluded in January 1921: 'The *fascio* would not have the great importance which it has acquired in the city of Bologna . . . if it had not attracted the sympathy and consensus of a majority of the citizens.'[39] In the first six months of 1921 the fascists destroyed 119 Chambers of Labour, fifty-nine Case del popolo (socialist cultural circles), 107 cooperatives, eighty-three offices of the Land Leagues (*leghe contadine*, associations of day labourers), socialist printing shops, public libraries, and mutual help societies, making a total of 726.[40] Between February and May 1921 (when the general election was held) socialist leaders were terrorised and beaten, in some cases murdered; socialist and labour cooperatives and employment offices lay in ruins. The punitive expeditions of the *camice nere* moved north to Mantua and the Veneto, and south to Bologna and Ravenna.[41] The movement spread to Tuscany and elsewhere, targeting specifically 'red' areas. Where the socialist vote was low, there was only sporadic violence.[42]

Violence paid off: Ferrara, hitherto a socialist stronghold, turned fascist at the national election of 15 May.[43] The bloodshed continued for the following year and a half – until the March on Rome. Italo Balbo, the leader of the Ferrara *fascisti*, described, with some satisfaction, the destruction and violence inflicted in the course of twenty-four hours in July 1922, 'destroying and burning down . . . offices and buildings belonging to socialists and communists. It was a terrible night. Our passage was marked by high columns of fire and smoke.'[44] 'Our objective', he explained, was 'to devalue the state, destroy the

The 'industrial triangle'

Areas of fascist violence between 1920 and 1992

present regime and all its venerable institutions. The more our actions are seen to be scandalous, the better.'[45]

The flavour of the rhetoric of the time – mimicking D'Annunzio – can be captured from a document of one of the many right-wing student groups that were springing up in Italy, the '*appello*' launched in April 1920 by the Consiglio nazionale dell'avanguardia studentesca:

> *If the War celebrated for us who are young the glorious epic tale of conscious youth springing from blood and ruins, from clashes and battles more scorching and red than the sun itself, for those of you who are even younger, the present twilight of mediocrity and base cowardice must not appear like the implacable grey of the autumn. You should feel it announcing the flight from darkness and the rise of a radiant dawn that will never know sunsets.*[46]

Who were the fascists in 1920–22? This is not easy to establish. According to their own calculation of November 1921, 24 per cent were 'rural workers', 15.5 per cent 'industrial workers', 13 per cent students (far in excess of the national average), 11.9 per cent small farmers, 14 per cent white-collar workers (much higher than the national average), and 9 per cent shopkeepers (equivalent to the national average). The substantial presence of rural and industrial workers was presumably due to recent fascist successes in wresting from the socialists the control of labour exchanges in many localities. Those who wanted employment would switch their allegiance from the socialists (or the *Popolari*) to the fascists. However, the main source of fascist support was certainly university and high school students. In 1921 there were 49,000 university students in Italy (5,000 of whom were women) and 136,000 high school students over the age of fifteen (one-third female). Thus the total male student population (high school and university) was nearly 135,000 – 19,000 of whom were active fascists, a much higher proportion than any other group in the population.[47]

These largely young, overwhelmingly male, activists clearly enjoyed their militaristic activities, their macho solidarity and comradeship, and their flirtation with the idea of martyrdom. For those who had undergone the experience it was like being at war again; for those who had missed it, it was a way of playing at being soldiers with far fewer risks than confronting well-equipped Austrian troops.[48] Those who had joined the movement in 1920 and 1921 were attracted by its negativity.[49] They were dismayed, but in different ways, by events, and joined the party which seemed to be against all the things they were against too – liberals, socialists, Catholics, Parliament, trade unions, Bolshevism and anything else that appeared to limit the freedom of these essentially lower-middle-class groups.

Though violence continued until the March on Rome, the peak was unquestionably the six months between the local elections of November 1920 and the May 1921 general election. In May 1921 Giolitti included the fascists in his electoral list, the *blocco nazionale*, thus legitimising them. After that the fascists played on two registers: violence and legality. Thus May 1921 was a key date in Mussolini's advent to power.

Why did Giolitti, who was Prime Minister during these six months of violence, not only fail to suppress the movement, but include it in his electoral list – the worst mistake of his political career? It is obvious that he totally underestimated them: 'The fascist candidates,' he asserted, 'will be like fireworks. They will make a lot of noise but will leave nothing behind except smoke.'[50] He was also faced with the fact that should the new election produce a hung Parliament as in 1919, the political crisis would escalate. There was also the realisation that he simply did not have the power to contain fascist violence.

During the months leading up to May 1921, fascism had acquired the unequivocal support and encouragement of landowners large and small. All those who hated socialism forgot their differences and cheered the *camice nere*; this included those of established wealth who were afraid to lose it, those who had acquired it and were eager to defend their status, and those who had lost money and prestige and who needed someone to blame. The liberalism of the Italian middle classes had always been skin-deep. Before the war, they trusted Giolitti and his ilk because there was no one else to trust. They had never embraced a love of democracy. Now all their frustrations, old and new, were coming to the fore. The plain-speaking fascists were going to clean up the place and re-establish some order. And if this required some tough action, so be it. As Mario Missiroli, the editor of Bologna's conservative daily *Il Resto del Carlino*, wrote at the time, the local bourgeoisie was distinguished by 'an absence of political sensitivity, decorum, and moral restraint'.[51] Yet it was the same Missiroli who had warned the agrarians in 1917: 'We see the agrarians standing by the wayside, cowering, timid, afraid to move ... Perhaps they do not know that an African wind is blowing from Russia ... Don't they realise that there are men in Italy capable of becoming Lenin? ... Haven't they become aware that a colossal union against landed property is being organised?'[52] Now the landowners were fully aware, and they had found their own Lenin.

Decisive to the success of fascism was the tacit or overt support of the local police and the *carabinieri* (the national paramilitary police corps). Often the army supplied the fascists with means of transportation. The growth of the fascist movement, writes Adrian Lyttelton, 'was powerfully assisted and sometimes even initiated by the regular army ... The higher ranks of the army continued to view the fascist movement with "cautious benevolence".' Government attempts to dissuade them were 'half-hearted'.[53]

Giolitti felt he could not contain fascist violence by military means. This was partly because he could rely on neither the forces of law and order nor the army.[54] He felt that the risk of not being obeyed far outweighed the consequences of doing what he had always done: whenever he had been threatened by a new opponent, he had chosen to share power rather than confront it. For him, what was happening was simply yet another chapter in the age-old conflict between landowners and workers.[55] He thus completely misunderstood the situation. This error was compounded when he dissolved Parliament and called a new election. He imagined that he could get the result he wanted, as he had done repeatedly in the years before the First World War. He also believed that the prospect of an election would lead to a diminution of violence. This did not occur. The violence escalated, as did the number of people killed.

The results, at first, appeared to justify Giolitti. The socialists plummeted to 24 per cent of the vote (from 32 per cent in 1919), and lost one-fifth of their seats (from 156 to 123). The left was thus more divided than ever, since the Communist Party obtained fifteen seats and just under 5 per cent of the votes. The PPI marginally improved on the 20 per cent of the seats it had obtained in 1919, gaining a further eight seats. The fascists won thirty-five seats in Giolitti's list. They were hardly a major force, and anyway, instead of supporting

Giolitti, they promptly joined the ranks of the opposition, with Mussolini taking his seat on the far right, aloof.

The fascists' greatest gains were made in provinces where the left also had its greatest support – that is, in areas where the clashes between left and right had been most acute.[56] The socialists, however, were still the largest single party, and the PPI was second. But the country was as ungovernable as ever, with a plethora of parties dividing among themselves the 535 seats of the Chamber of Deputies.

## Election of May 1921 (Chamber of Deputies)

| | Percentage of vote | Seats |
|---|---|---|
| Partito nazionale fascista | 0.5 | 2 |
| Blocchi nazionali (including fascist candidates) | 19.1 | 105 |
| Partito dei combattenti (veterans) | 1.7 | 10 |
| Partito economico | 0.8 | 5 |
| Partito democratico riformista | 1.8 | 11 |
| Partito democratico sociale | 4.7 | 29 |
| Partito liberale democratico | 10.4 | 68 |
| Partito liberale | 7.1 | 43 |
| Partito popolare italiano (Catholic) | 20.4 | 108 |
| Partito repubblicano italiano | 1.9 | 6 |
| Partito socialisti indipendenti (reformists) | 0.6 | 1 |
| Partito socialista | 24.7 | 123 |
| Communist Party (PCI) | 4.6 | 15 |
| Linguistic minorities lists (Slavs and German-speakers) | 1.3 | 9 |
| Others | 0.4 | 0 |
| | **100** | **535** |

The fascists entered Parliament 'flaunting their disrespect'.[57] But the acquisition of a semblance of political respectability came at a price. The truculent rhetoric which had accompanied fascism's meteoric rise had now to be mellowed by the art of moderation and compromise. It is here that Mussolini, hitherto an insignificant player in the drama of post-war Italian politics, came into his own. He may have been only thirty-seven at the time, but he had spent almost twenty years in a political *milieu*. He knew that his task was to calm down his more violent supporters without alienating them, and without sedating them so much that they would no longer be seen as a threat.

Giolitti's successor as Prime Minister was Ivanoè Bonomi, a former reformist socialist and ally of Bissolati. He had been Minister for War when fascist squads devastated the 'red areas', and had, directly and indirectly, tolerated fascist violence. Now, as Prime Minister, he was urging its end, appealing directly to Mussolini to come to an understanding with the socialists – what he labelled '*un patto di pacificazione*'.

Mussolini understood immediately that the time had come to play the moderate card. The *patto di pacificazione* was signed on 3 August 1921. Both sides undertook to desist from acts of violence towards each other. Mussolini had told his supporters that discipline and obedience to the leader were what mattered. Not all accepted this *dictat*. The more militant fascists, such as Dino Grandi and Italo Balbo, were furious, in part because they had obtained funds from local landlords to squash rural socialism and the job had not been finished. Mussolini threatened to resign. Then he declared that the time had come to transform his Fasci di combattimento into a proper political party:

*It is necessary to form a party, well-organised and disciplined, so that it is able, when required, to transform itself into an army capable of using violence defensively or offensively. This party must have a mind, that is a programme. Theoretical and practical assumptions must be reviewed, amplified and, if necessary, abandoned.*[58]

The grumblings, of course, continued, and so did the violence, but since there was no one else who could aspire to the succession and become fascism's leader, Mussolini was free to build on the credentials he had acquired with 'respectable' Italy. His position of ambivalence between fascism's intransigent and insurrectionary wing and its legalistic side was paying off – in politics it often pays to be vague.

It was only at this stage, just over a year before the March on Rome, that Mussolini appeared to develop a plan. It was important to build bridges with the various political and social forces that mattered in the country: the monarchy, the Church and the industrialists. With each he made his peace.

The first to be reassured were the industrialists. In one of his rare speeches in the Chamber of Deputies in 1921, Mussolini declared that fascist economic policy would be liberal and not socialist, even though fascism was not liberal, nor was it nationalist, or democratic, or Catholic. Fascism was fascism, he said, with an air of determination. 'This identification is a sign of strength ... Fascism is destined to represent in Italian history a synthesis between the indestructible theories of economic liberalism and the new forces of the world of labour.'[59] Until recently, he wrote in February 1922, the left had represented change and progress whilst the right represented reaction and conservatism, but now things had changed. The era of the left and of democracy (1848 to 1920) was over. While the nineteenth century was the century of revolution, the twentieth would be the century of restoration. Democracy was on the way out. Capitalism no longer needed democracy: 'The orgy of indiscipline was over.'[60]

What did the industrialists make of Mussolini? By 1922, after the March on Rome and Mussolini's appointment as Prime Minister most of them welcomed fascism, as did much of the liberal establishment. But did they do so because they were rich bourgeois, and had realised that fascists would be on their side? And did Italian capitalism actually require a strong authoritarian government? After all, industrialists do not all have the same interests. Some wanted protectionism and state intervention; others wanted *laissez-faire* and de-regulated markets. But, since their productivity was lower than that of their foreign competitors, they all wanted low wages. So there was a good reason to be against strikes, unions and socialists, and on the side of those who put down strikes, burned socialist buildings and regarded trade union members as traitors. Yet, insofar as industrialists were concerned, the period of emergency, when the socialists were growing stronger and the workers had occupied the factories, was over. By 1921 the 'reds' had been routed.

During the war most industrialists, especially those active in the chemical and steel industries, had been on the side of intervention and had financially supported the interventionist press, including Mussolini's. His *Il Popolo d'Italia* did receive help, but this was not particularly significant, and by 1920 the paper was struggling financially.[61] The industrialists could not trust Mussolini yet, since they all knew that he had been a socialist, and that he was still using socialist rhetoric. Mussolini realised this, and proceeded in the course of 1921 to modify his language in the direction of economic liberalism, abandoning most of the principles of state interventionism he had espoused earlier. By 1922, to all intents and purposes he had whole-heartedly embraced economic liberalism, obtaining the praise of the intransigently economically liberal Luigi Einaudi, who criticised the prefect of Bologna on 7 June 1922 for pandering to Bolshevism because he had tried to stop fascist violence.[62]

The *Corriere della sera* and Einaudi were equally impressed by Mussolini's Udine speech of 20 September 1922, when he declared:

> *We want to remove from the state all its economic powers. Enough of the state-railwayman, the state-postman, the state-insurer. Enough of the state maintained at the expense of taxpayers and endangering the exhausted finances of the Italian state. The police should remain, for they protect honest people from thieves and villains; the state-educator should remain, for the benefit of the new generations; the armed forces should remain, for they protect the borders of the Fatherland; and foreign policy should remain.*[63]

Yet this position was not entirely new. On 6 April 1920, in an article in *Il Popolo d'Italia* on the introduction of daylight saving time, Mussolini had launched into an anti-state tirade of a distinctly liberal flavour, though at the time hardly anyone had noticed it:

> *I too am against the new legal time because it represents another form of state intervention and coercion ... I start with the individual and proceed against the state ... The state, with its enormous bureaucratic machine, is asphyxiating. The individual could tolerate the state when it was simply a soldier and a policeman. But now the state*

*is everything: a banker, a money-lender, the owner of gambling houses, the pimp, the insurer, the postman, the railwayman, the entrepreneur, the industrialist, the school-teacher ... The state controls everything and causes nothing but harm: each of its activities is a disaster.*[64]

By 1922, of course, everyone took note of every word of Mussolini's. Ettore Conti was a bourgeois and an industrialist, and proud of it. In 1922 he was also a Senator and, more importantly, the president of the industrialists (the Confindustria). Until the end of 1921 his diary does not mention Mussolini. At the beginning of 1922, however, he noted with considerable satisfaction that the Italian masses seemed to have finally acquired a decent patriotic spirit, that the myth of Lenin was less strong among them, and that they were reacting against socialism and socialist violence.[65] Some of the credit for this must go, he thought, to Mussolini and his fascists:

*A man of such stature, who defends the fruits of victory; who is against the peasant leagues who abuse and threaten those who own property, their goods and their crops; who is the enemy of those who want to establish the rule of the Hammer and the Sickle; who has more trust in the élites than the masses; is made not to be disliked by the Confederazione Industriale ... I hope he and the fascists will participate in a government of greater authority than that of the mild [Luigi] Facta.*[66]

And when Mussolini finally became Prime Minister, Conti wrote: 'Provided he succeeds in forgetting where he came from and in obtaining the support of other parties he will be able to benefit the country.'[67] He might have been comforted by

Mussolini's famous interview to the *Manchester Guardian*, a week before the March, which seemed to seal the embrace between fascism and economic liberalism. His tone was reassuring: 'Our policies will be completely liberal.' A fascist government would inaugurate a new era of economic freedom, it would spend less and earn more, balance exports and imports even if it meant that Italians would have less to eat, and public expenditure would be reduced to a minimum.[68]

Before 1922, the industrialists either ignored fascism or were lukewarm about it. Throughout 1922 they were almost silent on the question of fascism. It is almost as if they were afraid to take sides, or could not quite bring themselves to support fascism openly.[69] As the fascists grew stronger, the industrialists joined the bandwagon, as did many others who had until recently preached the importance of democracy. By the time Mussolini was appointed Prime Minister, most capitalists turned to support him almost without reservations. On 29 October 1922 the Confindustria warmly approved the new government (before Mussolini's formal acceptance of his appointment).[70] In any case, the industrialists could no longer support Giolitti. His economic proposals when he was Prime Minister in 1921 had completely alienated them. His abolition of anonymity in share dealings caused even more alarm than his suggestion that war profits should be 'confiscated', probably because everyone knew that confiscation was out of the question, whereas abolishing anonymity in share dealings was a serious threat, since it would strike a blow at the widespread practice of avoiding taxes.[71]

This does not mean that the industrialists (or rather, their association, the Confindustria) had become pro-fascists. Their preferred government would have been one led by a liberal. It simply means that they too had come to terms with the widespread belief that not only should one not move against the fascists, but that one should compromise with them, since they had become the main anti-socialist force in the country.

This is what led many industrialists to declare, once Mussolini was ensconced in his prime ministerial chair, that this was the first time there had been a government that was clearly on their side.[72] And while many liberals soon had second thoughts, the industrialists became more enthusiastic. When Luigi Albertini, the editor of the *Corriere della sera*, joined the anti-fascist camp in 1923 (having reluctantly supported Mussolini in 1922), he met the hostility of the Confindustria, and was soon ousted. Luigi Einaudi was shocked that after the murder of the socialist deputy Giacomo Matteotti in June 1924 (see page 139) the industrialists had remained silent, continuing to hold the view that whatever misdeeds Mussolini or his supporters had committed, they were nothing in comparison to those the Bolsheviks would have carried out had they had the chance.[73]

After Mussolini became Prime Minister the industrialists were further compensated by having Alberto De Stefani, an intransigent economic liberal, appointed Minister of Finance – to the delight of Luigi Einaudi.[74] De Stefani reduced taxes, eliminated some tax exemptions which protected the poorer taxpayers, made share dealing and tax avoidance easier by reintroducing anonymity (abolished by Giolitti), eliminated rent control, privatised life insurance (introduced by Giolitti) and granted the management of the telephone system to the private sector. The fascists had been lucky to gain government at the end of the post-war economic crisis, which gave way to a substantial period of economic growth (manufacturing output increased by more than 50 per cent between 1921 and 1925. Only Japan grew faster).[75] Yet the industrialists continued to worry. They had been pleased by the abolition of the trade unions in 1925 and their replacement by fascist-controlled workers' organisations. However, these needed to maintain some sort of credibility with the workers who had been compulsorily drafted into them, and so could not behave as the industrialists would like them to behave. Thus the 'class struggle' never completely subsided – as the communist leader Togliatti pointed out.[76] But there was no ground for industrialists to worry excessively: wages were contained throughout the twenty years of fascism.

As Mussolini cultivated business, he also renounced all the last vestiges of his anti-monarchism, declaring that one could renew Italian politics without removing the monarchy, and that the monarchy had no interest in impeding the progress of the fascist revolution. 'We must have the courage to be monarchist,' he declared in Udine on 20 September 1922.[77] A few days before the March on Rome, at the rally organised by the fascists in Naples on 24 October 1922, he told his audience that there was no reason for the monarchy to be against them, because both fascists and monarchists were in favour of the unity of the country, and neither cared about democracy. Nor did the fascists wish to take away from the people their 'toy', that is to say, their Parliament – for most Italians this really was hardly more than a toy, since six out of eleven million voters did not bother to vote.[78] The audience dutifully shouted 'Long live the King!', underlining the commitment of the fascists to sustain the monarchy, a commitment enhanced by the fact that the monarchy was far more popular in the south, and particularly in Naples, than in the north. So it could not have been a surprise to them when Mussolini, upon arriving in Rome on 30 October 1922, shouted to the crowd: '*Viva il Re! Viva l'Italia! Viva il fascismo!*'[79]

The Church was more difficult to conciliate. But Mussolini tried. In his first speech to the Chamber of Deputies, on 21 June 1921, he announced that 'fascism does not preach anti-clericalism'; anti-clericalism was now an 'anachronism'; 'today the Latin and imperial traditions of Rome are represented by Catholicism'; 'the secular state should offer the Vatican all the material help required for schools, churches, hospitals etc.', provided the Vatican renounced temporal power. And for good measure he added that he was against divorce.[80] On the occasion of the death of Pope Benedict XV, Mussolini, in an article in *Il Popolo d'Italia* on 24 January 1922, respectfully noted the international position of the Catholic Church, looked forward to a reconciliation between the Italian state and the Vatican, and condemned the anti-clericalism of 'charlatans'.[81] A week later, in an interview with the *Resto del Carlino*, he regretted that the fall of the Bonomi government had made it difficult for the Chamber of Deputies to commemorate adequately the death of the Pontiff.[82] On 27 July 1922 he repeated that fascism was neither anti-religious nor anti-Catholic: 'Our position is far more subtle than the mediocre anti-clericalism of the pre-war period.'[83]

Reassuring the Church was only part of the operation. Equally important was reassuring the Catholic party, the PPI. But the PPI was deeply divided, another factor that turned to Mussolini's advantage. There was a 'left' Catholic tendency whose aims were a kind of social Catholicism based on the network of 'white' trade unions and cooperatives.[84] The objective of this tendency was to ensure that political Catholicism would evolve in direct competition with socialism (following the indications of the 1891 papal Encyclical letter *Rerum Novarum*). The white trade unions did not oppose the occupation of the factories in 1920, but did not support them either. Much firmer was the response of Catholics to fascist violence in rural areas. In response they were labelled 'white Bolsheviks', and their offices were attacked by the Blackshirts with almost as much vigour as those of the 'reds'.[85] The more centrist Catholics realised that some kind of common front with the liberals was necessary, but they remained strongly anti-Giolitti, partly because his decision to tax profits from share dealings would also penalise religious orders and the Vatican, but also because he was reluctant to give the white trade unions the same recognition he had been prepared to extend to those of the socialists.

Clearly, few had realised that by 1921 Italy was on the verge of the abyss. In fact the PPI, like the socialists, had no strategy and no plans. The death of Benedict XV deprived the party of its strongest protector in the Vatican. His successor, Pius XI, was a deeply conservative Lombard cleric, not enamoured of democracy and virulently anti-communist.[86] Vatican policy shifted gradually away from the PPI as the PPI haggled with the reformist socialists on matters such as education, hoping to entice them into supporting a liberal government. But events developed more rapidly than anyone had foreseen. The fascists grew in power and prestige. The Vatican exercised pressure on the PPI not to isolate itself, thus paving the way for the PPI's formal assent to the new Mussolini government at the end of October 1922.

By 1922 Mussolini found himself in an unusually favourable situation. The socialists had been damaged by the occupation of the factories and were split; the liberals were no longer able to form a government; the Catholics were divided. The violence inflicted by the fascists on the countryside had been widely supported, and they had been rewarded with seats in Parliament. Mussolini was now regarded as a respectable statesman. Still reacting to other people's mistakes, he avoided making any of his own. He did his best to ensure that the rougher elements in his party were never in a position of dictating policy, and warned them that the fascists were 'an election party', ready to take part consciously in electoral contests.[87] He insisted that though fascism could not support the existing Italian state, it would support it to avoid a 'socialist state' or an 'anarchistic anti-state'.[88]

The *fascisti* were teaching the Italians, and particularly the bourgeoisie, that violence was legitimate, since the state was too weak, corrupt and effeminate to impose its will, to use the monopoly of force it possessed. Thus a parallel state had to be set up, not to destroy the old one, but to stiffen its mettle. In his speech to local fascists in Milan on 4 October 1922, Mussolini explained that the 'liberal state' was now 'only a mask behind which there is no face; a scaffolding behind which there is no building, a force without a spirit'.[89]

It was because the authorities and the middle classes tolerated violence that the fascists continued to use it, unpunished, throughout 1922. When, on 3 August, the fascists took over Palazzo Marino – the city hall of Milan – and expelled the socialist council, the local magistrate, Antonio Raimondi, was instructed not to intervene.[90] Milan had been run by socialists for a number of years, but it was also the commercial and financial centre of Italy and the 'bourgeois' city *par excellence*. The *Corriere della sera*, regarded as the organ of the Milanese financial and commercial élites, reported the whole violent act with no word of condemnation.

At the beginning of October 1922 the fascists also occupied Trento and Bolzano, forcing the resignation of the government-appointed local prefect. The government failed to respond. When, in the summer of 1922, the Socialist Party called for a strike urging a return to legality (the *sciopero legalitario*), the fascists moved to suppress it, substituting themselves for the authorities in order to re-establish their own 'order'. Still more scared of the 'reds' than of the 'blacks', the old establishment rallied behind them. Antonio Salandra noted in his memoirs that 'all classes interested in public order' had no doubts, 'rightly or wrongly', that fascism was the last valid fortress against anarchy and subversion.[91]

The willingness of the state to tolerate fascists' acts of violence, repeated illegalities, the wearing of uniforms and their posing as a state within the state began to astonish even the fascists themselves. One of Mussolini's most loyal and close supporters, Cesare Rossi, wrote that if Italy had a government worthy of the name it would have sent the police and the *carabinieri* to disband them. It was not conceivable, he continued, that a state, which had its own army and police, could allow the existence of armed bands with their own military-style hierarchy and regulations: 'This proves that in Italy there is no state. It's useless; we are forced to take over. Otherwise the history of Italy would become a joke.'[92]

The fascists appeared to be the masters of Italy, ready to do the dirty work on behalf of a frightened bourgeoisie. The *Corriere della sera* alternated between a general embarrassment at their 'excesses' and a resigned acceptance that thuggish elements had to do the job the dominant classes were unable and unwilling to perform. A leading article by Luigi Albertini, the editor, in August 1922 condemned the socialist 'legalitarian' strike in words of fire ('an enormous disaster visited upon the entire nation') which he never used against the fascists.[93] Of the liberal press only Turin's *La Stampa* remained firmly on the side of legality.[94] The Milan-based *Corriere della sera* was then the main paper in Italy, selling some 450,000 copies and widely regarded as the voice of the enlightened and 'modern' bourgeoisie. Its editor, Albertini, a leading interventionist since 1915, detested Giolitti, whom he often accused of aiming to establish a dictatorship in Italy and of having tried to keep Italy out of the war. When Mussolini launched his movement in 1919, the *Corriere* – in an article on 23 March, noted with some satisfaction that he had been an interventionist. Subsequently, however, the rare mentions of fascism were relegated to the section of the newspaper dedicated to 'local news', and were often accompanied by reminders to readers that this was a movement aimed against Leninist threats and propaganda.[95]

By April 1921 Albertini was saluting fascism as 'the most extreme expression of a resurgent national consciousness' – not a full endorsement, but not a criticism either.[96] Throughout 1922 the *Corriere* regarded the socialists and not the fascists as the main threat to the country, and demanded a 'strong' government.[97] It repeatedly blamed the socialists and not the fascists for violence,[98] declaring that the fascists were simply responding to socialist violence, that if only the government dealt effectively with the socialists there would be no further need for the fascists to mouth revolutionary slogans,[99] and that in any case the fascists had no desire to impose a dictatorship.[100] In September the tone became increasingly pro-fascist. The fascists – the *Corriere* wrote – had accepted economic liberalism, and were far more open-minded than the socialists.[101] The paper rejoiced at Mussolini's Udine speech because it recognised the fundamental democratic principles of the state.[102] On 6 October the *Corriere* published on its front page a reassuring interview with Michele Bianchi, the Secretary General of the Fascist Party, who, when asked whether the fascists were preparing a coup, exclaimed: 'A military march on Rome? A *coup d'état*? ... Who has ever conjured up such fantasies? It is, of course, quite true that we are discussing a march on Rome, but it would be a spiritual march, entirely legal.'[103]

But the *Corriere* was now getting worried. The fascists had occupied Trento and Bolzano. Mussolini had started talking about a new fascist state while the paper was still defending the Liberal state, what it called 'the spirit of the Occident'.[104] What was the solution? In a leading article entitled 'An Atmosphere of Crisis' the paper noted that there was a division inside the government between those who wanted to move firmly against the fascists and those who thought they could be prevailed upon to refrain from violence. The paper sided with the latter, adding that perhaps the fascists could be persuaded to join the government.[105] From then on the *Corriere della sera* insisted that the only solution was to bring the fascists inside the ruling coalition – even before Mussolini had suggested it openly.

By the time the second government of Luigi Facta, the last before fascism, had been installed on 10 August 1922, the fascists had imposed their will, obtaining the resignation of local prefects in a whole array of towns in central Italy. By October the Fascist Party had, to all intents and purposes, become a 'counter-state' with its own 'army' (the Milizia) and uniforms. The fascist daily *Il Popolo d'Italia* even published, on 3 October, the 'regulations' of the Milizia. Had there been a functioning Italian state it would have disbanded the Milizia, using its army and its police force. But Facta's government was a government in name only: 'We need a stronger government,' *un governo più forte*, thundered a leading article in the *Corriere della sera*.[106] The cry for stronger government was now picked up by the vast majority of liberals. The former Prime Minister, Nitti, in a speech given ten days before the advent of Mussolini, made the case for it with characteristic realism: 'Italy spends too much,' he explained; 'she spends more than she produces.' Sacrifices were needed, there should be no strikes in the public sector, people should have faith in the market, and above all the country needed a strong government – it did not matter 'whether it is of the left or of the right'.[107]

# FIVE

# 'We Need a Strong Government'

What alternatives were there to bringing the fascists into the ruling coalition? Was there any chance of an anti-fascist government of national unity based on an alliance between the socialists and the PPI – the main anti-fascist parties? By the beginning of 1922 the seriousness of the political crisis had become so manifest that some socialists were convinced of the necessity of seeking an alliance with the *Popolari* of the PPI. But the socialists – as we have seen – were so divided that had the reformists sided with the Catholics, the maximalists would have regarded it as confirmation of their belief that the reformists had become indistinguishable from the bourgeois parties. And reformists and *Popolari* together were not strong enough to form a government. It was necessary to involve the maximalists too. But these were too dogmatic to take such a step.

Would the *Popolari* have been amenable to such an unlikely partnership? They and the socialists, after all, were facing the same enemy, since both had been trying to organise the rural masses and both had been subjected to fascist violence. But it was never seriously thought that Don Sturzo and Filippo Turati could be in the same government, even though some of their followers envisaged such an agreement.[1] Some local pacts did occur, notably in Bergamo (August 1921) and Cremona (March 1922), but the leadership of both the PSI and the PPI refused to sanction a national one.[2] And in July 1922, while Luigi Facta was trying to save his first government (he had succeeded the hapless Ivanoè Bonomi in February 1922) and was negotiating with the *Popolari*, the fascists destroyed the home in Cremona of the local leader of the 'left' *Popolari*, Guido Miglioli. Facta condemned the violence, but did nothing to prevent it. The *Popolari* brought down the government, but they continued to negotiate. As for the socialists, Miglioli was a 'bluff', a 'trick', and a servant of the employers.[3]

Don Sturzo, the leader of the PPI, could have signed a pact with Turati, but he would have been denounced by the Vatican, which had come to regard Mussolini as acceptable once he had discarded his anti-clericalism with the nonchalance with which one might discard an old pair of slippers, useful when new but embarrassing when old.[4] This is why, on 25 September 1922, in preparation for the local elections in Milan, the PPI joined an amorphous 'national bloc' alongside liberals, nationalists and fascists in order to prevent the possibility of a socialist mayor.

The division inside the Socialist Party reached its peak in the few weeks before Mussolini's advent to power, when it held its congress in Rome. Just as the 'bourgeois bloc' was about to be united under the banner of fascism, the left was in disarray, and what was worse, did not realise it. The maximalist majority, though not quite ready to side with the communists and join Lenin's Third International, had decided that the time had finally come to break with the reformists and expel them.

So there were now three parties of the left in Italy: the Communist Party (formed in 1921), the Socialist Party under the maximalist leader Giacinto Serratti, and the new reformist

Partito socialista unitario under Filippo Turati and Giacomo Matteotti. Had the left been united, it would have remained the largest party in the Parliament, and had it been able to conclude a pact with the Partito popolare, there would have been an anti-fascist majority. The divisions inside the socialist camp were not just about rival personalities, but were caused by genuine doctrinal and political differences. So a united Socialist Party was impossible. The maximalists were right when they accused the reformists of deluding themselves: the time for convincing the more enlightened part of the Italian bourgeoisie (represented by Giolitti and Francesco Saverio Nitti) to embrace reforms had gone. Such options no longer existed.

It was not only the socialists who were divided. The PPI too oscillated between a 'social' wing, which sought to organise Catholic workers and peasants and which had had to face fascist violence, and the more 'political' wing, led by Don Sturzo, closer to the Vatican.

The liberal establishment was equally in disarray, particularly after the fall of the first Facta government in July 1922. None of the grand old men of the Liberal Party was keen to fight for the succession. During the crisis Giolitti remained in Vichy, taking the waters. This is why Luigi Facta, the most reluctant of Prime Ministers (and a loyal protégé of Giolitti), was reappointed by the King – much to the despair of his wife Maria, who wrote to her daughter that she could not wait for 'Dad' to be free of politics, an activity he found increasingly 'repugnant'.[5] By 21 October – a week before the March on Rome – Facta's correspondence with his wife (tired of Rome, she had returned to Pinerolo in Piedmont) reveals a man desperate to give up power to a man (Mussolini) desperate to have it: 'I have great hopes to be free of all this in the next few days ... Oh darling ... the day I will leave I shall be indescribably happy.'[6] By then the liberals had run out of alternatives.

No stand against fascism could be expected from the nationalists, since their main goal had been to stop the socialists entering the government – and not just the maximalists, but even the moderate Turati socialists who would press for a pacifist foreign policy.[7] The permissive attitude of the nationalists towards fascism was understandable. Fascism, to them, was not a real danger, since all the fascists' violent activities were directed against those who appeared to threaten the established order – which included anyone on the left. They also realised, and rightly so, that Mussolini's foreign policy would not depart in the slightest from that prescribed by the nationalists themselves – a course of action that would shake Italians out of their complacency and their inferiority complex *vis-à-vis* the rest of 'advanced' Europe. These conservatives shared with the country's élites an almost 'desperate wish' to become 'modern'.[8] They regarded their country and most of their countrymen as culturally backward, not ready for the enlightened reforming social liberal democracy which they thought existed in countries they regarded as the true models of advanced Europe (Great Britain and France).

Nationalists, like the intellectual élites, did not really like the Italian people. D'Annunzio had wanted a greater Italy because he was deeply dissatisfied with the existing one. The futurist poet Marinetti regarded Italians as weak and feeble (too much pasta, he thought). On their own the conservatives had never been strong enough to impose an authoritarian path towards modernity *à la* Bismarck. The old Piedmontese state was certainly centralist, but nothing like Prussia. There had been previous attempts to impose authoritarian regimes – Prime Ministers such as Luigi Pelloux and Francesco Crispi restricted civil liberties – but these were often defeated. The conservatives thus looked benignly upon Mussolini. Perhaps he would succeed where they had failed, and teach the lower classes their place in the wider order of things. The fact that Mussolini himself belonged to those classes was a positive advantage. In the end, the conservatives believed, he would do as he was told, much as the task of the butler is to instil a sense of decorum and discipline among insolent and restless servants. The Italian ruling classes had already made their choice in favour of authoritarian repression. Even Giolitti, worried about the looming public spending deficit, was openly negotiating with Mussolini.[9] But the maximalists (and the communists) were wrong too: revolution may have had a chance in 1919, but certainly not in 1921, let alone in 1922, when the left could no longer control events.

True liberals were out of action as well. Their leading light, Luigi Einaudi, remained obtuse to the last. As Italy was staring into the abyss, one week before the March on Rome he was worrying about the use of taxpayers' money to rescue some shipyards, instead of leaving things to the wonders of the market.[10]

As Piero Gobetti wrote in *La Rivoluzione liberale* (1924), Italian liberalism had failed to produce a proper political ruling class, a proper class of entrepreneurs and a proper liberal consciousness. The liberals, he explained, were unable to reform the country because they were only in office, never fully in power. Their main preoccupation was to hold on to office by means of ruses and clever tricks. Italian liberals, he added – disarmingly, since he was a liberal himself – had no passion for freedom.[11] This was quite an indictment, but the truth was worse. The main failure of Italian liberalism was that it was never able to create an economic environment favourable to the middle classes, who had been kept out of every single centre of power, whether political, bureaucratic or cultural. They felt unrepresented and undervalued. They were not committed to any form of democracy, since the only one they knew seemed to protect the interests of the rich. In fact few in Italy were committed to democracy: not the traditional liberals (although they used the word 'democracy' at every opportunity), not the nationalists, not the fascists, not the maximalists, not the communists, and not the Catholics.

The fascists found themselves almost trapped by a success they had not entirely foreseen. The respect they had acquired when they broke the socialists' 'legalitarian' strike in August 1922 caught them by surprise. No one had tried to stop them, while the socialists, who had called the strike in the hope that it would rally all those in favour of law and order against extremists, were completely isolated. Supporters flocked in greater numbers than ever before to the Fascist Party. As Michele Bianchi, the Secretary General, explained at a meeting of the party's central committee in August 1922, the movement had become so big that it would have to be used 'either to strengthen the state or it would have to become the state. It could no longer remain outside the sinews of power.'[12]

This convinced Mussolini to contemplate a march on Rome. He announced it as a possibility well before anything had been planned.[13] The actual decision, according to Italo Balbo's memoirs, was taken on 16 October 1922 at a meeting in Milan attended by Mussolini and Michele Bianchi.[14] But already in early September Mussolini was regularly announcing that fascism was about to assume its 'responsibilities': the government of the country.[15] On 26 September Mussolini spoke in Cremona, with the local fascist boss Roberto Farinacci at his side. To a rapt crowd, in a silence which the reporter of *Il Popolo d'Italia* called 'absolute' and 'religious', he announced that fascism had started a march which would not 'stop until we have reached our goal: Rome'.[16]

Further planning occurred on 24 October, at the conference of the Fascist Party. This had been convened with the help of the authorities, who even provided discounted tickets so that delegates could reach it by special trains. The plan was to occupy buildings in northern and central Italy. Then three armed columns would gather at three points on roads outside the capital. That this was conceived as a way of exercising pressure was made evident by Mussolini himself. Wearing a black shirt with decorations on his sleeves, he entered the crowded hall greeted by three blasts of a trumpet. The enthusiasm, according to press reports, was 'enormous'. Then, as 'total silence' descended, he declared: 'We have come to Naples from all parts of Italy for a ritual of fraternity and love ... The whole of Italy is looking to us because since the war there has not been a phenomenon more interesting, more global, more powerful than Italian fascism ... We have created our myth. This myth is faith and passion ... It does not have to be reality ... Our myth is the Nation, the greatness of the nation.'[17]

The Naples meeting was more a festival than a party conference. The 'delegates' paraded for three hours, called themselves 'legions'; many wore uniforms and sang war songs. In the popular areas of the city the crowds observed the show, congregating on balconies and monuments and along the roads. Mussolini now talked openly about which ministries he wanted: Foreign Affairs, War, Navy, Labour, and Public Works, although he claimed that 'I do not want to take part in the government myself.'[18] These were the same ministries he had mentioned on 20 October in his interview with the

*Manchester Guardian* and to the former Prime Minister Antonio Salandra on the previous day.[19]

The Naples conference was attended by various Neapolitan Senators, including the philosopher Benedetto Croce. Their attendance did not imply consent, let alone support: it was normal for local dignitaries to attend such events.[20] But it did signify that the fascists were regarded as a normal and legitimate party. The President of the Chamber of Deputies, Enrico De Nicola, sent Mussolini a formal message: 'To you and all the colleagues who participate, my personal and cordial message of best wishes.' This did not make Mussolini's tone any more conciliatory. Amidst encouraging cries of 'To Rome! To Rome!' he intoned: 'Either they will give us the government or we will take it by descending upon Rome. It is a question of days, hours perhaps ... Go back to your towns and await our call. Orders, if necessary, will be given. In the meantime, break ranks and express your solidarity with the armed forces: *Viva l'Esercito! Viva il fascismo! Viva l'Italia!* ... We fascists do not want to enter government from the back door. In the end it may well be force that decides, for in history, force decides everything.'[21]

Mussolini went back to Milan. The organisers planned the march and Luigi Facta, the Prime Minister, decided, finally, to act. With the agreement of the cabinet he prepared a decree announcing a state of siege and the introduction of martial law. The government assumed that the King would sign it, and that consequently the march would be stopped by the army. But Victor Emmanuel III did not sign the decree. Instead he asked Mussolini to form the next government.

Much has been written about the King's refusal to sign. Here was a true historic moment, one in which a single decision taken by a single person could have changed the course of history. Or so it was thought. But one should also ask another question: why did Facta prepare a decree, since by then so much of respectable public opinion, as well as the majority of the establishment, had decided that it was impossible to govern without the fascists? Perhaps Facta's action could be seen as a last-minute attempt to control fascism, divesting it from its extra-legal element, blocking the march and then enabling a new government to be formed, possibly one led by his patron, Giolitti, in which the fascists would have an important but secondary role. If this is accurate, then the task of the March was not that of starting a revolution, but the far more prosaic and far less exciting one of preventing a compromise with the old Giolitti establishment. In this case the March would merely have been a way of exercising pressure in the familiar parliamentary game to which Italians had grown accustomed.

And why did the King refuse to sign?[22] It is true that Victor Emmanuel III was malleable, and did what his advisers told him to do. Now those advisers were divided, and he had to make up his own mind. Making up his mind was one of his problems. He was a man with few qualities. He lacked physical attractiveness, self-assurance and imagination. His short stature was an added burden, particularly as he was often surrounded by tall military officers. Victor Emmanuel was born in 1869 in Naples, where he lived throughout his child-hood and early adolescence, away from the royal court in Rome. He grew up without brothers or friends of his own age, and developed a taciturn personality. Unlike his father, King Umberto I, and his grandfather Victor Emmanuel II (the first King of Italy), who boasted that they had never read a book, he liked reading, though like them he received a military edu-cation. His real lifelong passion, however, was numismatics, an occupation which caused much amusement and mockery.

Council of Four at the Versailles Peace Conference. From left: David Lloyd George, Vittorio Orlando, Georges Clemenceau and Woodrow Wilson.

*From left*: King Victor Emmanuel III, Giovanni Giolitti, General Armando Diaz and Admiral Thaon de Revel. The latter, an early supporter of Mussolini, became Minister for the Navy in Mussolini's first government.

*Above left*: Victor Emmanuel III (1869–1947). He ascended the throne in 1900 after his father, Umberto I, was assassinated by an anarchist. He appointed Mussolini Prime Minister in 1922 and dismissed him in 1943. He abdicated in May 1946, just as Italy was poised to become a republic.

*Above*: Giovanni Giolitti (1842–1928). He dominated Italian politics in the first two decades of the twentieth century. An enlightened liberal, he was prime minister five times. He believed he could co-opt the fascists the way he had often done with those who had opposed him in the past.

*Left*: Luigi Albertini (1871–1941). Editor of the prestigious liberal Milan daily *Corriere della sera* from 1900 to 1925. A staunch anti-socialist, he at first supported Mussolini's advent to power. He soon repented, but was sacked in 1925.

*Above*: Filippo Turati (1857–1932). One of the founders of the Italian Socialist Party, he was the leader of its reformist wing until, just a few weeks before the March on Rome, he was expelled from the party. He continued to oppose Mussolini until 1926, when he was forced into exile.

*Above right*: Luigi Sturzo (1871–1959), a Sicilian priest who founded the Catholic Partito Popolare Italiano in 1919. Close to the Vatican, he was more anti-socialist than anti-fascist. Once fascism was consolidated he chose to live in exile in England, and later in the USA. He returned to Italy after the Second World War.

*Right*: Luigi Facta (1861–1930) was Prime Minister twice in 1922, both times reluctantly, standing in for his political patron Giovanni Giolitti. Unable and unwilling to stand up to mounting fascist violence, he gave way to Mussolini in October 1922.

Italo Balbo (1896–1940), looking at his most respectable on the steps of St Paul's Cathedral in London in 1930. In 1921 he had been one of the most violent leaders of the Blackshirts in the Emilia. Later he became Minister for Aviation and Governor of Libya. He died in a crash landing at Tobruk.

Rome, November 1921. The fascist movement becomes a party: the Partito Nazionale Fascista. Mussolini is at the table in the foreground, turned towards the camera.

28 October 1922: the March on Rome. Most of the fascist 'revolutionaries' carried little more than sticks and old rifles.

The first marchers arrive in Rome under the benevolent stare of police and passers-by.

Mussolini as he is about to enter the Quirinale Palace and become Prime Minister. He is accompanied by Giacomo Acerbo, who later drafted the electoral law that ensured that any coalition gaining a simple majority would be rewarded with 66 per cent of the seats.

Pope Pius XI (1857–1939). He became Pope in February 1922, eight months before the advent of fascism. In 1939 he signed the Vatican Treaty, thus ending the dispute (extant since the unification of Italy) between the Roman Catholic Church and the Italian state.

Giacomo Matteotti (1885–1924). Leader of the reformist socialists in Parliament, he denounced fascist violence in a famous speech in the chamber in 1924. He was murdered shortly afterwards. There is no absolute certainty that Mussolini ordered the assassination, but those convicted of the crime were amnestied after only a few months.

FIFTEEN CENTS

July 20, 1936

# TIME

*The Weekly Newsmagazine*

*Underwood & Underwood*

Volume XXVIII

**DUX**
*"It is our peace, Roman peace."*
(See FOREIGN NEWS)

Number 3

Circulation Office, 350 East 22nd Street, Chicago. (Reg. U. S. Pat. Off.) Editorial and Advertising Offices, 135 East 42nd Street, New York.

Mussolini regularly appeared on the covers of major international news magazines, as here, in July 1936.

In 1896 Francesco Crispi, then Prime Minister, in pursuit of vague designs in the Balkans, arranged for Victor Emmanuel to marry Jelena (Elena) Petrović-Njegoš, the daughter of the King of Montenegro. The wedding took place without fanfare – the Pope, still hostile to the kingdom of Italy, had refused to grant the use of St. Peter's Cathedral for the ceremony.

Victor Emmanuel III came to the throne unexpectedly early, at the age of thirty-one, in July 1900, after his father was murdered by the anarchist Gaetano Bresci. In the first decade of his reign he had the good fortune to have as Prime Minister someone as clever as Giolitti. A British ambassador wrote of the young King: 'He is thought to have ideas but has never propounded them to anyone.'[23] His closed persona, difficult to decipher, was also noted by others.[24] He seldom interfered in politics, not even in foreign policy, though the constitution explicitly granted him significant powers in this domain.

With hindsight, this was the man who was to decide whether Italy would remain a democracy or become a dictatorship. But only with hindsight, for what looks epoch-making to those who come after does not always seem so dramatic to contemporaries. Looking back, one can say that the King made a fateful decision; but at the time, that decision did not appear to be leading to a dictatorship. Victor Emmanuel did not understand that by refusing to sign the decree, he had shown his hand. He thought that he was simply avoiding risks. Before asking Mussolini to form a government he had wanted to appoint Salandra. But Salandra had understood the situation. He said he would not accept unless he could bring Mussolini into the government, and he told everyone the same thing: fascist leaders such as Cesare Maria De Vecchi and Dino Grandi, as well as Mussolini himself. He was relieved when he was told that Mussolini had turned down the offer of a ministry for himself. He, Salandra, was off the hook.[25] By then Mussolini must have been thinking that he had not designed this complex political choreography, culminating in a march, just to give Salandra the top job. As he wrote in his newspaper: 'Our victory appears to be complete with the almost unanimous consensus of the country. But our victory cannot be mutilated by last-minute compromises. A Salandra government would not have been worth our mobilisation. The government must be clearly fascist.'[26] Mussolini had realised that he could go for the ultimate prize. The gamble had paid off. He could not be stopped. And if 'they' were not going to stop him, it was because they had realised he was too strong.

The real question, then, is not why did the King not sign, but why he should have signed. Let us examine the issue from his point of view. He was faced with some unpalatable facts. It is true that the fascist march could have been easily disbanded, but it was an equally unassailable fact that it was generally assumed that the next government would have to include fascist ministers, perhaps as many as five. Liberal public opinion had already come to terms with the idea that it was necessary to negotiate and compromise with the fascists, offer them jobs and ministries, involve them in a coalition. Few outside the left had demanded that they should be physically crushed. Even fewer expected this to happen, since so little resistance had been offered previously. The entire liberal establishment was in agreement: the *Corriere della sera*, former Prime Ministers such as Giolitti and Salandra, the President of the Chamber of Deputies, Enrico De Nicola, the respected philosopher Benedetto Croce, the liberal economist Luigi Einaudi, and even the Church. Salandra, who had been asked by the King whether he had been right not to sign, agreed, telling him, 'One proclaims a state of emergency when one has the will and the means. This was not the case.'[27]

And if Victor Emmanuel had signed, he still would have had to find someone willing to lead a government with fascist ministries, while Mussolini would have kept himself out of it, with the option of bringing down the government at a time of his own choosing. The King could not have forgotten that he had been unable to find a liberal willing to serve after the resignation of the first Facta government, and that he had been obliged to reappoint Facta. The only alternative was Giolitti; but Giolitti might have tried to implement a programme of advanced social reforms with the support of the *Popolari* and some of the socialists. This was, however, improbable, and in any case was unacceptable to 'liberal' Italy. Indeed, Giolitti had completely ruled out his candidature as early as July 1922,[28] though of course few believed him, and the *Corriere della sera* still feared his return as late as 24 October. The *Corriere* and Luigi Albertini, speaking on behalf of the *bien-pensant* consensus, had no doubts: better, far better, the coarse Mussolini, than liberal Italy's great statesman, who was eighty by then and whom the King had never liked. The King was also aware that there were many fascist sympathisers at court, including his own mother and his dashing cousin Emanuele Filiberto, Duca d'Aosta, a handsome war hero, the darling of the veterans – and rumoured by some to be more than willing to take over the crown should Victor Emmanuel decide to abdicate.

Though there was no real 'March on Rome', and no 'fascist revolution' in the sense that there was a Russian Revolution, the combination of unchecked fascist violence with a general feeling of appeasement among the establishment meant that a psychological climate had been created which would have made it improbable that the fascists could be militarily crushed. And while the King could rely on the armed forces and on General Pugliese, he was aware that the fascists had considerable support among the top echelons of the military, who would have been upset to be forced to move against Mussolini. He probably consulted some high-ranking generals, such as the pro-fascist Tahon di Revel, who would have advised him to 'give in' before the fascist advance (Tahon di Revel was compensated with a ministry in Mussolini's government).

As Marco Mondini explained: 'The politicisation of the officer corps, suspicions concerning the loyalty to the institutions of many of that corps' commanders, the fear that ordinary Italian soldiers might follow the example of the Bolsheviks, all converged to make the army an unreliable instrument in the eyes of the civilian leadership.'[29] Was not appointing Mussolini the more reasonable and 'softer' option?

As far as the King was concerned, the real enemy was on the left, above all the vociferous maximalists who still dreamed of revolution. By taking a firm stand against fascism, the King would have legitimised resistance to it, and hence would have favoured the left. Faced with the dilemma of opting for a shift to the right or one to the left, the King chose Mussolini, who unlike the socialists had made repeated conciliatory gestures towards the monarchy. Perhaps he could be placated by being put in charge. Then he would have a stake in the existing system, would calm his troops and restore law and order. Besides, even if the fascist threat had been eliminated, would Italy have been any more governable? Would Parliament have been any less paralysed? Would not this give more space to the maximalist wing of the Socialist Party, encourage the reds and make the fascists even more determined to take over completely – and on their own terms? The fascists did not have many votes or many MPs, but their party was on the rise, a pole of attraction for the young and the hot-headed. Mussolini was preferable to the thugs surrounding him, and he, and he alone, seemed able to contain them. Stopping the march would have given the establishment only a temporary respite. The fascists might have regrouped, revived anti-monarchist feelings, and been ready to fight another day.

The King's decision to ask Mussolini to form a government was accepted by virtually the entire political establishment, including the liberal press. Only Luigi Salvatorelli in the pages of *La Stampa* lamented the turn towards illegality, towards a state of exception which might last longer than people thought (prescient words).[30] The industrialists were overjoyed, particularly when they found out that Alberto De Stefani, a fascist committed to liberal economic policies, had been appointed as Minister of Finance (he turned out to be too much of an economic liberal for featherbedded industries such as chemicals and armaments). The liberals lined up to be included in Mussolini's government; the Catholics did the same, with the support of the Vatican, which conveniently forgot that only three years previously, Mussolini had de-manded the sequestration of Church property. The liberal group in Naples, to which Benedetto Croce belonged, sent Mussolini a telegram of good wishes.[31]

What surprises in the events leading to 30 October and its aftermath is the absence of any kind of mass movement. Milan, reported the *Corriere della sera*, was 'calm and almost normal'. The city centre – from where cars and bicycles had been banned – was under the control of the military and the *carabinieri*.[32] The trade unions, exhausted, were quiet, as were all the organisations of civil society in Italy. There were no strikes, no counter-demonstrations. As Mussolini remarked in his speech to the Chamber a few weeks after the March: 'If the Italian working class had wanted to launch a general strike it would have been a problem for us.'[33]

The only ones who were mobilised were the fascists themselves, and even they functioned purely as props in a game entirely played at the top. The left had little to say, except that Mussolini was simply another expression of capitalism. The communists were weak, and almost indifferent to a situation they knew they could not influence even minimally. Though industrialists and the press talked of the Bolshevik peril, there was in fact not the slightest danger from the left, whose supine role was that of being used to justify Mussolini's rise to power. As De Felice has suggested, Italy was tired: three and a half years of war, two years of social unrest, an economic crisis, and fascist violence.[34] All people wanted was peace and quiet.

Not many – including fascists – realised what was actually happening: that a new regime was being born, that soon there would be no more elections, and no more press freedom. The majority in the liberal camp saw no urgent reason (and no political advantage) to oppose Mussolini. If he failed, it would be his failure, and they might reap the benefits. They had been prepared to tolerate numerous acts of violence, and were soon to accept a severe curtailment of rights and liberties, because each curtailment by itself was eminently defensible, and could always be seen as temporary and due to special circumstances. So, when Mussolini took over there was a chorus of approval, oscillating between outright enthusiasm (the nationalists and the right in general), and resigned acceptance of it as a necessary evil (the liberals). Even someone like Giovanni Amendola, a liberal whose distaste for Mussolini was virulent, thought in November 1922 that it was necessary to vote in favour of the new government in order to prod it along on the way to legality and constitutionality. Moderate socialists like Anna Kuliscioff thought exactly the same. Gaetano Salvemini, who soon turned against fascism, thought that Mussolini was no worse than other Italian 'dictators' (he meant elected Prime Ministers like Crispi and Giolitti), and that if he were to free Italy of 'old mummies and bandits' (*vecchie mummie e canaglie*) 'he would have achieved something useful for the country'.[35] Salvemini, whose anti-fascism was not in doubt, wrote that 'Mussolini is not as mad as the hordes of fascist youths.'[36]

Once Mussolini was appointed Prime Minister, the fascists camping outside Rome were allowed to enter the city. The event was described by the *Corriere della sera* with the reassuring headline 'The Homage of the Fascists to the Unknown Soldier and to the King'.[37] The 'revolutionaries' assembled in the gardens of Villa Borghese, paraded in via Nazionale and via del Tritone and gathered in Piazza del Popolo. Their leaders informed them that now that the objective had been reached, it was necessary to avoid any acts of violence. They had to behave: 'Place flowers in the barrels of your guns and be gentle with the local population which has welcomed you so visibly.' Since many of the marchers were war veterans they marched in perfect order, cheered the Duce, broke discipline only to vandalise the homes of some socialists, and went home.

The belief that Mussolini would soon metamorphose into an ordinary politician, albeit one with populist overtones, had some foundation. The young journalist turned rabble-rouser had become Prime Minister after only a few years of agitation. He did not have the slightest experience of managing anything, and had been in Parliament for just over a year. All of a sudden he found himself in charge of a politico-bureaucratic machine which had been functioning on behalf of the same political élite for over sixty years. He could easily have become its prisoner, and turned himself into a mere figurehead. But it is also true that in 1921 and 1922 he had made hardly any tactical mistakes, and his few uncertainties and hesitations were caused by the objective difficulty of making decisions in an inherently unstable situation. Some of his collaborators, such as Aldo Finzi, who accompanied him on the train journey to Rome and was by his side when he accepted the King's appointment, had to stiffen Mussolini's resolve and urge him not to settle for anything less than full powers. Outwardly he had to behave as a sure-footed and decisive *Dux*, a leader always in control of everything, always sure of himself – but this was not always the case, and at times he was prey to self-doubt. This, to our contemporary politicians, constantly under the glare of the media, is a familiar predicament, but it was not so at the time. Then politicians did not have to play to a gallery and did not have to worry about their public image. Paradoxically, the future dictator knew that in the age of democracy one has to pander to the masses and indulge them.

He also had to cajole his hardbitten supporters. His in-augural speech as Prime Minister, on 16 November 1922, was blood-curdling, yet his words of utter contempt for Parliament were received with masochistic applause by all and sundry, except for the far left:

> *Gentlemen, what I am performing today in this Chamber is a formal act of respect, but I do not require in exchange any corresponding act of special recognition. Just as in May 1915 the views of the Chamber had been ignored, so now, in October 1922, a government has arisen without parliamentary approval. I should warn you all that I am here to*

*defend and develop the revolution of the Blackshirts, who will become a force for the growth, progress and standing of the nation. I could have won completely* (stravincere). *But I set limits to myself . . . With 300,000 armed youth ready for anything and waiting mystically for my command, I could have punished all those who had talked ill of fascism and had attempted to drag it into the mud. I could have transformed this grey and gloomy chamber into a bivouac for my platoons . . . I could have locked up Parliament and formed an exclusively fascist government. I could have, but, at least for now, I have not wanted to.*[38]

Luigi Einaudi, whose main concern was that the new government should follow 'classic economic' policies, was pleased. Italy was on the right path, he claimed.[39] But other liberals began to have misgivings. Luigi Albertini, the editor of the *Corriere della sera*, had already felt 'humiliated' and 'heartbroken' (his word) when his paper was banned on Sunday, 29 October.[40] Mussolini's speech added to his doubts: 'My conscience tells me that fascist reaction had saved Italy from the danger of socialism, which more or less openly, and more or less threateningly, had poisoned our lives in these last twenty years . . . But to re-establish the authority of the state, was it necessary to destroy it first and impose with force a Mussolini government?'[41] Still, hope dies hard and Albertini was still under the illusion that there were serious divisions within fascism, between those like Mussolini, 'who thinks that the state has at its disposal all it needs to maintain law and order, and those fascists who think that a kind of permanent revolutionary vigilance is necessary'.[42]

By then it was almost too late. During the next five years the basic structures of the fascist state were erected while those of the liberal state were dismantled. The first to go was the system of proportional representation, which had given excessive power to the socialists and the PPI. It is true that the Mussolini government had an unusually large majority, since it excluded only the left, and was supported by everyone else, including the *Popolari* (though seventeen of them left the Chamber rather than vote in favour of the government).[43] But Mussolini's own party was only a small element of this majority. He knew that he would not have got where he had without threats, and he continued to threaten Parliament: 'Who could stop me from shutting down Parliament?' he demanded in a speech on 27 November 1922. 'Who could have stopped me from proclaiming a dictatorship? Who could resist me, resist a movement which consisted not of 300,000 members, but 300,000 guns . . .'[44]

With remarkable rapidity Mussolini ensured himself a secure power base in Parliament (while 'resolving' the parliamentary crisis which had brought him to power). A new electoral law was introduced. The *legge Acerbo* (named after the MP who introduced it, Giacomo Acerbo) was passed in July 1923. Only the left voted against it, though some *Popolari* abstained. The new law established that the electoral list which obtained the most votes (not necessarily a majority) would be given two-thirds of the parliamentary seats. If the list was a coalition of several parties, the largest of these parties would get extra seats. A race took place to be in Mussolini's list. Most of the liberals – including Giolitti – joined in. The *Popolari* split three ways, but the majority voted in favour of the Acerbo Law. In the general election held on 6 April 1924 Mussolini's *listone* (the Big List) obtained 65 per cent of the votes and 375 MPs. The fascist-led coalition won by a landslide. There was now a formidable majority in Parliament, and one largely under the control of Mussolini. A new élite had come to power. Eighty per cent of fascist MPs were new, and two-thirds of them were under forty years of age. The old liberals had been routed, even Salandra barely managing to get himself elected.[45] Mussolini had not wanted to take risks. Though the fascists had been assured of victory, the electoral campaign had been marred by irregularities and violence, and the police refrained from intervening. To be on the safe side Mussolini had started a huge purge of the police, forcing forty commissioners and three hundred deputy commissioners to take early retirement.[46]

Violence continued unabated. In April 1924 the socialist reformist deputy Giacomo Matteotti made an impassioned speech in the Chamber denouncing not only the violence which had accompanied the election, but also the rapidly spreading corruption involving those near to Mussolini, including his brother Arnaldo. He was kidnapped and killed, perhaps on the orders of Mussolini himself.[47]

The murder of Matteotti proved to be the last straw for many Italian liberals, including Luigi Albertini. But the last straw had arrived too late. On 3 January 1925 Mussolini made a fateful speech in the Chamber. He declared, famously, that if violence had been the result of a particular political, moral and historic climate, then he, and he alone, had the responsibility since he, and he alone, had created this climate.[48] Of course, he had not created it on his own. The 'climate', to use his word, had been created by a complex historical process which Mussolini had been able to exploit, but he would not have been able to do so had Italy's élites not sought to use it for their own ends. But they now stood helpless as the man they thought would be their creature emerged as the true winner. In the following few years the old political parties that had ruled Italy were dissolved (the legislation was drafted by the nationalist jurist Alfredo Rocco), the trade unions were forced to amalgamate into the Confederazione nazionale dei sindacati fascisti, a Special Tribunal for the Defence of the State was created to deal with opponents and dissidents, the press was muzzled, a secret police (the Organizzazione di vigilanza repressione dell'antifascismo, or OVRA) was established, a new legal code was introduced, and school textbooks were placed under strict state control.

On 16 March 1928 a new law was introduced authorising the Grand Fascist Council to decide the list of all parliamentary candidates. Giolitti was the only one to speak out against it. It was his last speech in the Chamber. He died a few months later, at the age of eighty-six, realising perhaps – far too late – how catastrophic had been the political itinerary of the Liberal Party he had served all his life. In 1934 the Chamber, now useless, was abolished.

Mussolini could point to real achievements too. In foreign policy Italy obtained Fiume, thanks to the Treaty of Rome with Yugoslavia of 27 January 1924.[49] In February 1929 the Italian state made its peace with the Vatican, signing the Concordat. This pact recognised the Vatican State as an independent sovereign state, provided for compensation to be paid to the Church for the losses it suffered in 1870 when Rome was annexed to the Italian state, recognised Catholicism as 'state religion' and established the teaching of Catholic doctrine in all state schools. No wonder Pope Pius XI called Mussolini the man 'Providence has sent us'.[50]

In spite of its commitment to liberal economic policies, one of the first actions of the government was to save Ansaldo, one of the largest industrial corporations in the country, and the Banco di Roma from their financial troubles, and in so doing to rescue the myriad of Catholic banks which depended on the Banco di Roma, to the plaudits of the Vatican.[51] Italy's international position improved. A steady stream of American loans helped the stabilisation of the lira. By end of 1924 the state deficit had been wiped out, and the economy was growing (as was that of the rest of Europe). The 'international community', to use a contemporary expression, had no problems doing business with Mussolini. The British press was overwhelmingly favourable, although some papers began to have misgivings when they realised that the 'strong government' the Italians apparently needed had turned into a dictatorship. Not so the *Daily Mail*, which in 1928 saw in Mussolini the 'Napoleon of modern times'. Churchill, having met the Duce that same year, declared himself 'charmed', and said that had he been an Italian, he would have been 'wholeheartedly' with Mussolini from the beginning.[52] George Macaulay Trevelyan, the leading British historian of Italy, and a great liberal, conceded during a lecture he gave in 1923 that Mussolini was 'a great man' who, he hoped, would not destroy democratic institutions but would give his country 'order and discipline', explaining that it was difficult for Italians – unlike the British – to appreciate general elections.[53]

Churchill and Trevelyan were far from being fascist sympathisers, but, however briefly, they were prepared to accept fascist rule and Mussolini's assumption of power as 'inevitable'. As many often do, they organised the facts at their disposal according to a narrative familiar to them, one which had sustained them in their belief that Britain had produced a form of state and an empire which was the envy of the world, and which could not easily be exported. Italy had turned out to be a 'failed' state which could not be governed in the traditional way. It would either sink in complete chaos or emerge reinvigorated by a strong leader and a new regime. If the choice was chaos or resurrection, men of reason would opt for the latter – as did Trevelyan and Churchill, and the world in general. As the fascist dictatorship was established a step at a time, each step could be defended on its own terms, with no reference to the wider political or historical context. Many Italians accepted such terms. To them Mussolini's Italy was no worse than what had preceded it. Life continued to be easy or difficult, but politics had little to do with it. What does it matter if one can no longer vote, if no visible difference ensues? What does it matter if the press is muzzled, if one never reads a newspaper? At least now there was a leader telling them to be proud of being Italian, and promising a radiant future. And if the future was the same as the past, few would be disappointed, since most expected little from the political class in charge of their destinies. Only when the regime led the country into a new war, and demanded sacrifices for which they had not been prepared, did the majority of Italians turn against fascism. A war one does not win is never popular.

The gradual – if speedy – way in which the dictatorship was established, and the difficulty in defending what had taken place previously, made Mussolini appear to be the lesser evil. It made him appear more grandiose than he really was – a kind of *deus ex machina* descending upon the political stage to resolve all problems.

In real history, there are no miracles. Whatever happens is always somewhat connected to what happened previously. Mussolini could not have made history unless he had been made by history, unless the multiple processes which had brought about Italian unification and ensured the survival of the Italian state until the First World War had not come to be unravelled during the war and the political crisis that followed.

And the crisis, as Gramsci wrote, was an interregnum between the old society and the new one struggling to be born – a period in which 'a great variety of morbid symptoms appear'.[54] Mussolini was one of those. But some credit is due to him too. He appeared to be effortlessly superior to all his Italian political contemporaries, and to a large extent he was. Though he was constantly prey to self-doubt, the image he conveyed was that of a man possessed by a ferocious optimism, an absolute conviction that history was on his side – and the image is often what matters most. His liberal and conservative opponents lacked such conviction. They somehow suspected that they belonged to the old world, and as they clung to the sinking ship with desperation, they soon realised that the man they had entrusted with the task of saving them had his own project, and that it was quite different from theirs. The communists too thought that history was on their side, but their notion of history was long-term, a concept they used in order to survive at times of defeat, so as to avoid sinking into despair.

On the tenth anniversary of the March, the Mostra della rivoluzione fascista – the Exhibition of the Fascist Revolution – was opened in Rome. Posters, art, photographs and historical documents described the events leading to Mussolini's seizure of power and the achievements of his regime.[55] As often happens in such reconstructions, everything appeared to be linear, each event leading inexorably to the next; each step on the ladder dutifully positioned above the preceding one. But that is not how history proceeds. Mussolini could have been stopped, but those who could have stopped him – the liberals, the left, the Church, the monarchy – were unable or unwilling to do so, and walked, as if blindfolded, towards twenty years of dictatorship.

# NOTES

## Chapter 1: The Conjuncture

1 Italo Balbo, *Diario 1922*, Mondadori, Milan 1932, p.4

2 Giovanni Giolitti, *Discorsi extraparlamentari*, Einaudi, Turin 1952, p.345

3 Benito Mussolini, *Opera Omnia*, edited by Edoardo and Duilio Susmel, La Fenice, Florence 1951–1963, Vol. 18, p.464

4 *Corriere della sera*, 31 October 1922

5 Giovanni Gentile, *Che cosa è il fascismo. Discorsi e polemiche*, Vallecchi, Florence 1924, p.123

6 Augusto Turati, Preface to *Partito nazionale fascista. Le origini e lo sviluppo del fascismo attraverso gli scritti e la parola del Duce e le deliberazioni del P.N.F., dall'intervento alla marcia su Roma*, Libreria del littorio, Roma 1928, p.xv, henceforth *Partito nazionale fascista*

7 Cited in Antonino Répaci, *La marcia su Roma*, Rizzoli, Milan 1972, p.18

8 Mussolini, *Storia di un anno*, 1944, cited in Répaci, *La marcia su Roma*, cit., p.17 and also in Renzo De Felice, *Mussolini il fascista. La conquista del potere 1921–1925*, Einaudi, Turin 1966, p.307n

9 *Corriere della sera*, 31 October 1922

10 Vinicio Araldi, *Camicie nere a Montecitorio: storia parlamentare dell'avvento del fascismo*, Mursia, Milano 1974, pp.162–3

11 Emanuele Pugliese, *Io difendo l'esercito*, Rispoli, Naples 1946, p.30

12  Denis Mack Smith, *Italy and its Monarchy*, Yale University Press, New Haven and London 1989, p.250

13  'L'esercito nei giorni della "Marcia su Roma": dalle memorie storiche della 16ª Divisione di Fanteria di stanza a Roma nel 1922' in *Storia Contemporanea*, Vol. 15, No. 6, December 1984, p.1209

14  De Felice, *Mussolini il fascista*, cit., pp.324–5

15  'L'esercito nei giorni della "Marcia su Roma" . . .', p.1208

16  Mario Piazzesi, *Diario di uno squadrista toscano 1919–1922*, Bonacci editore, Rome 1980, pp.245, 51

17  Cited in Répaci, *La marcia su Roma*, cit., p.455

18  Ibid., p.414

19  Giulia Albanese, 'Dire violenza, fare violenza. Espressione, minaccia, occultamento e pratica della violenza durante la Marcia su Roma' in *Memoria e Ricerca*, No. 13, May–August 2003, p. 59

20  Balbo, *Diario 1922*, cit., p.185

21  *Corriere della sera*, 31 October 1922

22  Ibid.

23  *Partito nazionale fascista*, cit., p.140

24  In 'Lettere aperte a Mussolini' published in *Il Popolo d'Italia* (1920–21) collected in Gioacchino Volpe, *Guerra Dopoguerra Fascismo*, La Nuova Italia, Venice 1928, pp.261–6. Volpe joined the fascists in 1921

25  Benedetto Croce, *Nuove pagine sparse*, Vol. 1, Riccardo Ricciardi editore, Naples 1949 pp.62–3

26  Pierre Milza, *Mussolini*, Fayard, Paris 1999, p.9; Richard J.B. Bosworth, *Mussolini*, Arnold, London 2002, p.46

27  Martin Clark, *Mussolini*, Pearson Longman, Harlow 2005, p.9

28  Benito Mussolini, *Il mio diario di Guerra (1915–1917)*, Imperia, Milano 1923, p.80

29  De Felice, *Mussolini il fascista*, cit., pp.10–11

30  Marco Palla, 'La presenza del fascismo. Geografia e storia quantitativa' in *Italia Contemporanea*, No. 184, September 1991, p.400

31 Palmiro Togliatti, *Lectures on Fascism*, Lawrence and Wishart, London 1976, pp.15, 24–5

32 *Corriere della sera*, 1 November 1922; Gianpasquale Santomassimo, *La Marcia su Roma*, Giunti, Florence 2000, p.74

33 Reported by Massimo Rocca, once an anarchist then one of Mussolini's early supporters, expelled from the party in May 1924 in his *Come il fascismo divenne una dittatura. Storia interna del fascismo dal 1914 al 1925*, ELI, Milan 1952, pp.117, 122

34 Lenin, *Left-Wing Communism: an Infantile Disorder*, in *Collected Works*, Vol. 31, Progress Publishers, Moscow 1966, p.85. Emphasis in the original

35 Terry Pinkard, *Hegel. A Biography*, CUP 2000, p.228

36 See articles in *L'Ordine nuovo*, 19 August and 23 August and 1921, in Antonio Gramsci, *Selections from the Political Writings 1921–1926*, Lawrence and Wishart, London 1968, pp.61–5

37 Antonio Gramsci, leader in *L'Ordine nuovo*, March 1924 (unsigned) in Gramsci, *Selections from the Political Writings 1921–1926*, cit., p.212

38 Max Weber, *Economy and Society. An outline of interpretative sociology*, Vol. 1, University of California Press 1978, p.241

39 Paul Preston, *Franco. A Biography*, HarperCollins, London 1993, pp.364–8, 371

40 Paul Corner, 'The Road to Fascism: an Italian *Sonderweg*?' in *Contemporary European History*, Vol. 11, No. 2, 2002, p.274

## Chapter 2: A Divisive War – a Lost Victory

1 Hew Strachan, *The First World War*, Vol. 1: *To Arms*, OUP 2001, pp.110, 142

2 Ibid., p.150

3 Keith Robbins, *The First World War*, OUP 1984, pp.1, 17

4 Strachan, *The First World War*, cit., pp.110, 151

5 Adrian Gregory, 'British "War Enthusiasm" in 1914. A

Reassessment' in Gail Braybon (ed.), *Evidence, History and the Great War*, Berghahn Books, New York and Oxford 2003, pp.69ff

6  Ibid., p.79

7  Jean-Jacques Becker, *1914: Comment les Français sont entrés dans la guerre*, Presses de la fondation nationale des sciences politiques, Paris 1977, pp.279, 297, 307; see also Strachan *The First World War*, cit., p.142

8  Adolf Hitler, *Mein Kampf*, Hutchinson, London 1969, p.148

9  Strachan, *The First World War*, cit., p.104

10  Ibid., p.141

11  Peter Gay, *Freud*, Macmillan, London 1989, pp.348–9

12  See David Bidussa, *Il mito del bravo italiano*, il Saggiatore, Milan 1994

13  Immanuel Kant, *Observations on the Feeling of the Beautiful and Sublime*, trans. by John T. Goldthwait, University of California Press 1991, pp.98–100; originally *Beobachtungen über das Gefühl des Schönen und Erhabenen* 1794

14  Christopher Duggan, *Francesco Crispi*, OUP 2002, pp.707–8

15  Ronald S. Cunsolo, 'Libya, Italian Nationalism, and the Revolt against Giolitti' in *The Journal of Modern History*, Vol. 37, No. 2, June 1965, p.197

16  Pierfrancesco Morabito, 'Movimenti artistici e società di massa: il futurismo italiano' in *Italia Contemporanea*, No. 150, March 1983, p.19

17  In *I futuristi*, anthology edited by Francesco Grisi, Newton, Milan 1994, p.29

18  Paul Arpaia, 'Constructing a national identity from a created literary past: Giosuè Carducci and the development of a national literature' in *Journal of Modern Italian Studies*, Vol. 7, No. 2, 2002, p.193

19  John Mosier, *The Myth of the Great War*, Profile Books, London 2001, p.150

20  Great Britain, *Parliamentary Papers*, London 1920, LI Cmd. 671, Miscellaneous No. 7, 2–7

21  Piero Melograni, *Storia Politica della Grande Guerra*, Laterza, Bari 1969, p.2

22  Paolo Nello, *L'avanguardismo giovanile alle origini del fascismo*, Laterza, Roma-Bari 1978, p.9

23  Giovanna Procacci, 'Gli interventisti di sinistra, la rivoluzione di febbraio e la politica interna italiana nel 1917' in *Italia Contemporanea*, No. 138, 1980, p.51n

24  Mussolini, *Il mio diario di Guerra (1915–1917)*, cit., pp.203–4

25  Melograni, *Storia Politica della Grande Guerra*, p.467

26  Jonathan Dunnage, *The Italian Police and the Rise of Fascism: A case study of the province of Bologna 1897–1925*, Praeger, Westport Conn. 1997, pp.71–3

27  Melograni, *Storia Politica della Grande Guerra*, cit., p.23

28  Extracts in Araldi, *Camicie nere a Montecitorio*, cit., p.44

29  Walter L. Adamson, *Avant-garde Florence. From Modernism to Fascism*, Harvard University Press 1993, pp.191–2

30  Melograni, *Storia Politica della Grande Guerra*, cit., pp.548–51

31  Giuseppe Capacci, *Diario di guerra di un contadino toscano*, Cultura editrice, Florence 1982, p.38, see also p.65

32  Ibid., p.97

33  Ibid., p.106

34  Arrigo Serpieri, *La Guerra e le classi rurali italiane*, Laterza, Bari 1930, p.45

35  George L. Mosse, 'The Two World Wars and the Myth of the War Experience' in *Journal of Contemporary History*, Vol. 33, No. 4, 1998, pp.494–6, 498, 508; see also, specifically on British soldiers, Joanna Bourke, *Dismembering the Male. Men's Bodies, Britain and the Great War*, Reaktion Books, London 1996, pp.144–53

36  Mosse, 'Two World Wars and the Myth of the War Experience', cit., pp.491–513

37  Luigi Salvatorelli and Giovanni Mira, *Storia d'Italia nel periodo fascista*, Einaudi, Turin 1956, p.15

38  Nello, *L'avanguardismo giovanile alle origini del fascismo*, cit., p.3

39  Bosworth, *Mussolini*, cit., p.119

40  André Tardieu, *The Truth about the Treaty*, Boobs-Merrill Co.,
    Indianapolis 1921, chapter three, available at http://www.lib.byu.
    edu/estu/wwi/comment/treatytruth/tardieu00tc.htm

41  H. James Burgwyn, *The Legend of the Mutilated Victory: Italy,
    the Great War, and the Paris Peace Conference, 1915–1919*,
    Greenwood Press, Westport Conn. 1993, p.253

42  Cited in Richard J.B. Bosworth, 'The British Press, the
    Conservatives and Mussolini 1920–34' in *Journal of
    Contemporary History*, Vol. 5, No. 2, 1970, p.167

43  Francesco Saverio Nitti, *Peaceless Europe*, 1922 available on
    http://www.gutenberg.org/files/10090/10090–8.txt

44  Douglas J. Forsyth, *The Crisis of Liberal Italy. Monetary and
    Financial Policy, 1914–1922*, CUP 1993, pp.7, 13

45  Domenico Preti, *Economia e istituzioni nello stato fascista*,
    Riuniti, Rome 1980, pp.27, 35

46  Burgwyn, *The Legend of the Mutilated Victory*, cit., p.302

47  Adrian Lyttelton, *The Seizure of Power. Fascism in Italy
    1919–1929*, Weidenfeld and Nicolson, London 1973, p.30

48  Forsyth, *The Crisis of Liberal Italy*, cit., p.217

49  Roberta Suzzi Valli, *Le origini del fascismo*, Carocci, Roma 2003,
    p.17

50  Roberto Vivarelli, *Storia delle origini del fascismo: l'Italia dalla
    grande guerra alla marcia su Roma*, Vol. 1, Il Mulino, Bologna
    1991, p.504

51  Cited in Lyttelton, *Seizure*, cit., p.16

52  Alfredo Bonadeo, *D'Annunzio and the Great War*, Fairleigh
    Dickinson University Press, Madison NJ 1995, p.125

53  Colin J. Fewster, 'A Question of Loyalty: Hugo von
    Hofmannsthal, Stendhal, D'Annunzio, and Italian Nationalism'
    in *Seminar: A Journal of Germanic Studies*, Vol. 42, No. 1,
    February 2006, p.24

54  This is Vivarelli's view in *Storia delle origini del fascismo*, Vol. 1,
    p.566, as well as that of Giorgio Candeloro, *Storia dell'Italia*

*Moderna*, Vol. 8, *La Prima Guerra Mondiale. Il Dopoguerra. L'avvento del fascismo*, Feltrinelli, Milano 1984, pp.291–2; both are based on Nitti's recollections

55   *Corriere della sera*, 18 August 1922


## Chapter 3: The Parliamentary Crisis

1   Jens Petersen, 'Elettorato e base sociale del fascismo italiani negli anni venti' in *Studi Storici*, Vol. 16, No. 3, 1975, p.635

2   On the class origins of the *sepolcristi* see Paul O'Brien, *Mussolini in the First World War. The Journalist, the Soldier, the Fascist*, Berg, Oxford 2005, p.20

3   Cited in Nino Valeri, *D'Annunzio davanti al fascismo*, Le Monnier, Florence 1963, p.20

4   Mussolini, *Opera Omnia*, Vol. 13, p.14

5   Ibid., p.15

6   Claudia Baldoli, *Bissolati immaginario. Le origini del fascismo cremonese. Dal socialismo riformista allo squadrismo*, cremonabooks, Cremona 2002, see inter alia pp.23, 63, 65

7   Ibid., p.50

8   Alceo Riosa, 'Le patriotisme dans le verbe' in proceedings of the conference *L'éloquence politique en France et en Italie de 1870 à nos jours*, Collection de l'École française de Rome, Rome 2001, pp.101–17

9   Mussolini, *Opera Omnia*, Vol. 4, pp.161–2

10  Silvano Montaldo, 'Il Parlamento e la società di massa' in *Storia d'Italia, Annali 17, Il Parlamento*, a cura di Luciano Violante, Giulio Einaudi, Turin 2001, pp.248–50

11  Maria Serena Piretti, *La giustizia dei numeri: Il proporzionalismo in Italia (1870–1923)*, Il Mulino, Bologna 1990, p.298

12  Vivarelli, *Storia delle origini del fascismo*, Vol. 2, cit., p.165

13  Angelo Tasca, *Nascita e avvento del fascismo: l'Italia dal 1918 al 1922*, Laterza, Bari 1967, pp.17–28

14  Serge Noiret, 'Il PSI e le elezioni del 1919. La nuova legge

elettorale. La conquista del Gruppo parlamentare socialista da parte dei massimalisti', *Storia Contemporanea*, Vol. 15, No. 6, December 1984, pp.1104–16, 1024

15  Giampiero Carocci, *Il Trasformismo dall'unità ad oggi*, Unicopli, Milan 1992, p.10

16  Gaetano Mosca, *Sulla teorica dei governi e sul governo parlamentare*, Tipografia dello Statuto, Palermo 1884, pp.302–3

17  Mosca, *Sulla teorica dei governi . . .*, cit., p.310

18  Paolo Farneti, *Sistema politico e società civile*, Edizioni Giappichelli, Turin 1971, pp.169 and 194–280

19  Ibid., pp.181, 246

20  Carocci, *Il Trasformismo dall'unità ad oggi*, cit., pp.13–15

21  On the historical roots of modern personalistic and clientelistic politics in Greece see George Th. Mavrogordatos, *Stillborn Republic: Social Conditions and Party Strategies in Greece 1922–1936*, University of California Press, Berkeley Cal. 1983

22  P. Nikiforos Diamandouros, 'Greek Political Culture in Transition: Historical Origins, Evolution, Current Trends' in Richard Clogg (ed.), *Greece in the 1980s*, Macmillan, London and Basingstoke 1983, pp.44–5

23  Giorgio Candeloro *Storia dell'Italia Moderna*, Vol. 6, Feltrinelli, Milan 1970, p.161

24  Denis Mack Smith, *Italy. A Modern History*, Michigan University Press, Ann Arbor 1959, pp.110–12

25  Carocci, *Il Trasformismo dall'unità ad oggi*, cit., p.23n

26  Francesco Crispi, *Scritti e discorsi politici (1849–1890)*, Unione Cooperativa Editrice, Rome 1890, p.567, speech at the Poleteama Garibaldi in Palermo, 19 May 1886

27  Ibid., p.575

28  Silvio Spaventa, speech in Valeri (ed.), *La lotta politica in Italia*, cit., p.145

29  Silvio Spaventa, 'Discorso contro la Conciliazione', 20 September 1886 in Valeri (ed.), *La lotta politica in Italia*, p.91

30  Giovanni Sabbatucci, *Il trasformismo come sistema*, Laterza, Roma-Bari 2003, p.50

31  Cited in Répaci, *La marcia su Roma*, cit., p.104

32  Petersen, 'Elettorato e base sociale del fascismo italiani negli anni venti', cit., p.628

33  Giovanni Giolitti, *Discorsi Parlamentari*, Vol. 2, Camera dei Deputati, Rome 1953, pp.626–9

34  Ibid., pp.630, 633; see also Giolitti's speech of 29 October 1899, p.1186

35  Alexander De Grand, *The Hunchback's Tailor. Giovanni Giolitti and Liberal Italy from the Challenge of Mass Politics to the Rise of Fascism, 1882–1922*, Praeger, Westport Conn. 2001, pp.85, 94–5

36  Umberto Levra, 'Il Parlamento nella crisi di fine secolo' in *Storia d'Italia, Annali 17*, Einaudi, Turin 2001, p.171

37  Petersen, 'Elettorato e base sociale del fascismo italiani negli anni venti', cit., pp.629–30

38  Levra, 'Il Parlamento nella crisi di fine secolo', cit., p.175

39  Emilio Gentile, *L'Italia giolittiana 1899–1914*, Il Mulino, Bologna 1977, pp.35–6

40  Renato Zangheri, 'Introduction', *Lotte agrarie in Italia. La Federazione nazionale dei lavoratori della terra 1901–1926*, Feltrinelli, Milan 1960, p.xxix

41  Giuliano Procacci, *La lotta di classe in Italia agli inizi del Secolo XX*, Riuniti, Rome 1978, pp.81, 84–5

42  Piretti, *La giustizia dei numeri*, cit., p.80

43  Giorgio Candeloro, *Il Movimento Cattolico in Italia*, Riuniti, Rome 1982, p.315

44  Mario G. Rossi, 'Democrazia, socialismo, imperialismo nell'Italia giolittiana' in F. Andreucci et al. (eds), *Lezioni di storia d'Italia 1848–1948*, Riuniti, Rome 1979, p.144

45  Piretti, *La giustizia dei numeri*, cit., p.156

46  Giuseppe Berta, *Il governo degli interessi. Industriali, rappresentanza e politica nell'Italia del nord-ovest 1906–1924*, Marsilio, Venice 1996, p.23

47  Berta, *Il governo degli interessi*, cit., p.15

48  Ibid., pp.17, 37

49  De Grand, *The Hunchback's Tailor*, cit., p.4

50  Gaetano Salvemini, *The Origins of Fascism in Italy*, Harper, New York 1973, p.78

51  Preti, *Economia e istituzioni nello stato fascista*, cit., pp.26–7

52  Lyttelton, *Seizure*, cit., p.12

53  Forsyth, *The Crisis of Liberal Italy*, cit., pp.59ff

54  Piretti, *La giustizia dei numeri*, cit., p.271

55  Tommaso Detti, *Serrati e la formazione del partito comunista italiano*, Riuniti, Rome 1972, p.24

56  Vivarelli, *Storia delle origini del fascismo*, Vol. 2, p.502

57  Petersen, 'Elettorato e base sociale del fascismo italiani negli anni venti', cit., p.635

58  Milza, *Mussolini*, cit., p.257

59  Candeloro, *Storia dell'Italia Moderna*, Vol. 8, p.309

60  Charles S. Maier, *Recasting Bourgeois Europe. Stabilization in France, Germany, and Italy in the decade after World War I*, Princeton University Press 1975, pp.154ff

61  Ibid., p.188

62  Paolo Spriano, *The Occupation of the Factories*, Pluto Press, London 1975, pp.60–1

63  Ibid., pp.96–106

64  Lyttelton, *Seizure*, cit., p.37

65  Paolo Spriano, *Storia del partito comunista italiano. Da Bordiga a Gramsci*, Einaudi, Turin 1967, p.79

66  Speech to his constituents, 16 March 1924 in Giolitti, *Discorsi extraparlamentari*, cit., p.341

67  Salvatorelli and Mira, *Storia d'Italia nel periodo fascista*, cit., p.106

68  Forsyth, *The Crisis of Liberal Italy*, cit., p.238

69  Berta, *Il governo degli interessi*, cit., pp.58, 64

70  Renzo De Felice, *Mussolini il rivoluzionario 1883–1920*, Einaudi, Turin 1965, pp.627, 633

71  Berta, *Il governo degli interessi*, cit., p.92

## Chapter 4: The Advance of Fascism

1 Antonio Gramsci, 'What is reaction?', unsigned article in the Piedmont edition of *L'Avanti*, 24 November 1920, now in *Selections from the Political Writings 1910–1920*, cit., pp.360–2

2 Palmiro Togliatti, 'Episodi della guerra civile in Toscana' in *Opere 1917–1926*, Vol. 1, Riuniti, Rome 1974, pp.228–30, originally in *L'Ordine nuovo*, 9 March 1921

3 Piero Gobetti, *Scritti politici*, Einaudi, Turin 1997, p.354

4 De Felice, *Mussolini il fascista*, cit., p.113

5 Mussolini, *Opera Omnia*, Vol. 15, pp.183, 233; see also O'Brien, *Mussolini in the First World War*, pp.29, 54

6 Serpieri, *La Guerra e le classi rurali italiane*, cit., p.267

7 William Brustein, 'The "red menace" and the rise of Italian Fascism' in *American Sociological Review*, Vol. 56, No. 5, October 1991, p.655

8 Serpieri, *La Guerra e le classi rurali italiane*, cit., pp.70, 126

9 Ibid., p.94

10 Ibid., p.148

11 Frank Snowden, *The Fascist Revolution in Tuscany, 1919–1922*, CUP 1989, pp.19, 24

12 Ibid., p.36

13 Serpieri, *La Guerra e le classi rurali italiane*, cit., pp.83–5

14 Zangheri, 'Introduction', cit., p.xcix

15 Anthony L. Cardoza, *Agrarian Elites and Italian Fascism. The Province of Bologna 1901–1926*, Princeton University Press 1982, p.273

16 Snowden, *The Fascist Revolution in Tuscany*, cit., pp.72–3

17 Alice Kelikian, *Town and Country under Fascism. The Transformation of Brescia 1915–1926*, Clarendon Press, Oxford 1986, p.108

18 Paul Corner, *Fascism in Ferrara 1915–1925*, OUP 1975, p.108

19 Adrian Lyttelton, 'The "Crisis of Bourgeois Society" and the

Origins of Fascism' in Richard Bessel (ed.), *Fascist Italy and Nazi Germany*, CUP 1996, p.16

20 Petersen, 'Elettorato e base sociale del fascismo italiani negli anni venti', cit., p.641

21 Dunnage, *The Italian Police and the Rise of Fascism*, cit., pp.120–1

22 Kelikian, *Town and Country under Fascism*, cit., p.109; Segrè, *Italo Balbo. A Fascist Life*, cit., p.57

23 Corner, *Fascism in Ferrara 1915–1925*, cit., p.110

24 Ibid., p.112

25 Cited in ibid., p.113

26 Ibid., p.115

27 Kelikian, *Town and Country under Fascism*, cit., p.111

28 Pier Paolo D'Attorre, *Novecento padano: l'universo rurale e la 'grande trasformazione'*, Donzelli, Rome 1998, pp.46–54

29 Ibid., pp.22–5

30 Snowden *The Fascist Revolution in Tuscany*, cit., p.3

31 Corner, *Fascism in Ferrara 1915–1925*, cit., p.115

32 Araldi, *Camicie nere a Montecitorio*, cit., p.80

33 Gramsci, *Selections from the Political Writings 1921–1926*, cit., p.373, originally 'The Monkey-People' in *L'Ordine nuovo*, 2 January 1921

34 Mussolini, 'Il fascismo e I rurali' in *Gerarchia*, No. 5, 25 May 1922, now in *Opera Omnia*, Vol. 18, pp.203–5

35 Tobias Abse, 'Italian Workers and Italian Fascism' in Richard Bessel (ed.), *Fascist Italy and Nazi Germany*, CUP 1996, pp.42–3

36 Claudio G. Segrè, *Italo Balbo. A Fascist Life*, University of California Press 1987, p.49

37 Cardoza, *Agrarian Elites and Italian Fascism*, cit., p.307

38 Mario Missiroli in *Il Resto del Carlino*, 18 July 1913 cited in Cardoza, *Agrarian Elites and Italian Fascism*, cit., p.208

39 Cardoza, *Agrarian Elites and Italian Fascism*, cit., p.308

40 Santomassimo, *La Marcia su Roma*, cit., p.26

41 Corner, *Fascism in Ferrara 1915–1925*, cit., pp.137–8
42 Dahlia Sabina Elazar, 'Electoral democracy, revolutionary politics and political violence: The emergence of fascism in Italy, 1920–21', *British Journal of Sociology*, Vol. 51, No. 3, September 2000, p.475
43 Segrè, *Italo Balbo. A Fascist Life*, cit., pp.55, 59
44 Balbo, *Diario 1922*, cit., p.109
45 Ibid., p.30
46 Cited in Nello, *L'avanguardismo giovanile alle origini del fascismo*, cit., p.159
47 Petersen, 'Elettorato e base sociale del fascismo italiani negli anni venti', cit., pp.655–9
48 The flavour of such excitement is well captured in the diary of a Blackshirt; see Piazzesi, *Diario di un fascista toscano 1919–1922*, cit.
49 De Felice, *Mussolini il fascista*, cit., p.115
50 Cited in Richard J.B. Bosworth, *The Italian Dictatorship. Problems and Perspectives in the Interpretation of Mussolini and Fascism*, Arnold, London 1998, p.41
51 Cited in Paolo Alatri, *Le origini del fascismo*, Editori Riuniti, Roma 1977, p.63
52 Cited in Cardoza, *Agrarian Elites and Italian Fascism*, cit., p.234
53 Lyttelton, *Seizure*, cit., p.39
54 Salvatore Lupo, *Il fascismo. La politica in un regime totalitario*, Donzelli, Rome 2005, p.104
55 De Grand, *The Hunchback's Tailor*, cit., p.240
56 Brustein, 'The "red menace" and the rise of Italian Fascism', cit., pp.652ff; Lyttelton, *The Seizure of Power*, cit., p.188
57 Bosworth, *Mussolini*, cit., p.157
58 Benito Mussolini, 'Verso il futuro', *Il Popolo d'Italia*, 23 August 1921
59 Cited in Araldi, *Camicie nere a Montecitorio*, cit., p.117
60 Mussolini, 'Da che parte va il mondo' originally in *Gerarchia*, No. 2, 25 February 1922, now in *Opera Omnia*, Vol. 18, pp.66–72

61 Piero Melograni, *Gli industriali e Mussolini, rapporti tra Confindustria e fascismo dal 1919 al 1929*, Longanesi, Milan 1972, p.12

62 'Contro la servitù della gleba', cited in Lupo, *Il fascismo*, cit., pp.113–14; see also more of Einaudi's praise for fascism in *Corriere della sera*, 6 and 27 September 1922; see also Roberto Vivarelli, *Il fallimento del liberalismo. Studi sulle origini del fascismo*, Il Mulino, Bologna 1981, p.311 and De Felice, *Mussolini. Il fascista*, cit., pp.241–2 and 329–33

63 Benito Mussolini, 'L'azione e la dottrina fascista dinanzi alle necessità storiche della nazione' in *Opera Omnia*, Vol. 18, cit., p.419 ; see also the report in *Corriere della sera* of 22 September 1922

64 Benito Mussolini, *Opera Omnia*, Vol. 14, p.397, originally in *Il Popolo d'Italia*, 'L'ora e gli orologi'.

65 Ettore Conti, *Dal taccuino di un borghese*, Garzanti, Milano 1971 (1st edition 1948), p.169; entry of 7 January 1922

66 Ibid., pp.169–70

67 Ibid., p.191, entry of 31 October 1922

68 Interview to the *Manchester Guardian*, 20 October 1922, also in Mussolini, *Opera Omnia*, Vol. 18, p.451

69 Berta, *Il governo degli interessi*, cit., pp.164–5

70 See text in Santomassimo, *La Marcia su Roma*, cit., p.96

71 Forsyth, *The Crisis of Liberal Italy*, cit., p.244

72 Melograni, *Gli industriali e Mussolini*, cit., pp.43–6

73 Ibid., pp.75–7

74 *Corriere della sera*, 28 October 1922

75 Melograni, *Gli industriali e Mussolini*, cit., p.50

76 Palmiro Togliatti, *Lectures on Fascism*, cit., p.68

77 Mussolini, *Opera Omnia*, Vol. 18, p.418

78 Ibid., pp.456–7

79 Ibid., p.471

80 Benito Mussolini, *Scritti politici*, Feltrinelli, Milano 1979, pp.203–4

81 Mussolini, *Opera Omnia*, Vol. 18, pp.16–18

82 Ibid., p.36, Interview in *Il Resto del Carlino*, 3 February 1922

83 Mussolini, *Opera Omnia*, Vol. 18, p.318

84 Candeloro, *Il Movimento Cattolico in Italia*, cit., p.418

85 Ibid., p.427

86 Ibid., pp.441–2

87 Speech in Milan 4 April 1922 at the conference of the Consiglio nazionale of the Fascist Party in Mussolini, *Opera Omnia*, Vol. 18, cit., p.140

88 'Stato, antistato e fascismo' in *Gerarchia*, No. 6, 25 June 1922, in Mussolini, *Opera Omnia*, Vol. 18, pp.260–1

89 Mussolini, *Opera Omnia*, Vol. 18, cit., p.436

90 Santomassimo, *La Marcia su Roma*, cit., p.28, citing Raimondi's memoirs *Mezzo secolo di magistratura* (1951)

91 Antonio Salandra, *Memorie Politiche 1916–1925*, Garzanti, Milan 1951, p.17

92 Cited in De Felice, *Mussolini il fascista*, cit., p.317

93 *Corriere della sera*, 2 August 1922

94 Répaci, *La marcia su Roma*, cit., p.210

95 Alessandro Pezzimenti, *L'avvento del fascismo attraverso le pagine del Corriere della sera (1919–1925)*, Tesi Università degli Studi di Milano, 2000–01, pp.13–15 accessed http://www.tesionline.com/intl/thesis.jsp?idt=6650

96 'L'appello al paese' in *Corriere della sera*, 8 April 1921

97 *Corriere della sera*, 4 August 1922

98 *Corriere della sera*, 5 August 1922

99 *Corriere della sera*, 6 August 1922

100 'I valori morali della tradizione politica. A proposito di dittatura' in *Corriere della sera*, 8 August 1922

101 See leading article 'Riabbeverarsi alla sorgente' in *Corriere della sera*, 6 September 1922

102 *Corriere della sera*, 22 September 1922

103 *Corriere della sera*, 6 October 1922

104 *Corriere della sera*, 7 October 1922

105 'Atmosfera di crisi' in *Corriere della sera*, 13 October 1922; see also leading article 'Vane giustificazioni' on 17 October 1922

106 Leading article, 'Verso la crisi extra-parlamentare' in *Corriere della sera*, 15 October 1922

107 *Corriere della sera*, 21 October 1922

## Chapter 5: 'We Need a Strong Government'

1 Danilo Veneruso, *La vigilia del fascismo. Il primo ministero Facta nella crisi dello stato liberale in Italia*, Il Mulino, Bologna 1968, pp.219, 228

2 John M. Foot, ' "White Bolsheviks"? The Catholic Left and the Socialists in Italy, 1919–1920' in *The Historical Journal*, No. 2, Vol. 40, 1997, p.429

3 Ibid., p.431

4 Candeloro, *Il Movimento Cattolico in Italia*, cit., pp.443–5

5 See text of letter written on 18 July 1922, in appendix to Répaci, *La marcia su Roma*, p.611

6 Cited in Répaci, *La marcia su Roma*, cit., p.87

7 Veneruso, *La vigilia del fascismo*, cit., p.263

8 Gobetti, *Scritti politici*, cit., p.921

9 'Un discorso di Giolitti a Cuneo. Un invito ai fascisti – Un monito per la situazione finanziaria' in *Corriere della sera*, 24 October 1922 followed by the text of Giolitti's speech

10 Luigi Einaudi, 'Discordia felice' in *Corriere della sera*, 22 October 1922

11 Gobetti, *Scritti politici*, cit., pp.958–64

12 Cited in Répaci, *La marcia su Roma*, cit., p.331

13 See his interview to *Il Mattino* on 11 August 1922 in Mussolini, *Opera Omnia*, Vol. 18, cit., p.349

14 Balbo, *Diario 1922*, cit., p.178

15 See for instance *Il Popolo d'Italia*, 7 September 1922, in Mussolini, *Opera Omnia*, Vol. 18, cit., p.391

16 Lupo, *Il fascismo*, cit., p.119

17  *Corriere della sera*, 25 October 1922; also Mussolini, *Scritti politici*, cit., p.221

18  *Corriere della sera*, 25 October 1922

19  Interview to the *Manchester Guardian*, 20 October 1922 in Mussolini, *Opera Omnia*, Vol. 18, p.451, Salandra, *Memorie Politiche 1916–1925*, cit., p.19

20  Fabio Fernando Rizi, *Benedetto Croce and Italian Fascism*, University of Toronto Press 2003, p.41

21  *Corriere della sera*, 25 October 1922

22  Various hypotheses are ably examined by Répaci, *La marcia su Roma*, cit., pp.489–509

23  Mack Smith, *Italy and its Monarchy*, cit., p.147

24  De Felice, *Mussolini il fascista*, cit., p.311

25  Salandra, *Memorie Politiche 1916–1925*, cit., pp.22–5

26  De Felice, *Mussolini il fascista*, cit., p.374

27  Salandra, *Memorie Politiche 1916–1925*, cit., p.23

28  Giolitti, *Discorsi extraparlamentari*, cit., p.334

29  Marco Mondini, 'Between subversion and coup d'état: military power and politics after the Great War (1919–1922)' in *Journal of Modern Italian Studies*, Vol. 11, No. 4, December 2006, pp.457–8

30  Répaci, *La marcia su Roma*, cit., p.571

31  Rizi, *Benedetto Croce and Italian Fascism*, cit., p.45

32  *Corriere della sera*, 28 October 1922

33  *Corriere della sera*, 18 November 1922

34  De Felice, *Mussolini il fascista*, cit., pp.388–9

35  Ibid., pp.393–5

36  Cited in Bosworth, *Mussolini*, cit., p.180

37  'L'omaggio dei fascisti al Milite Ignoto e al Re' in *Corriere della sera*, 1 November 1922

38  Speech to the Chamber of Deputies in Mussolini, *Opera Omnia*, Vol. 19, p.17

39  Luigi Einaudi, 'Sulla buona via' in *Corriere della sera*, 18 November 1922

40 Leading article, *Corriere della sera*, 30 October 1922

41 *Corriere della sera*, 27 November 1922

42 Leading article, 'Lo stato forte', in *Corriere della sera*, 17 December 1922

43 *Corriere della sera*, 19 November 1922

44 Speech on 27 November, reported in the *Corriere della sera*, 28 November 1922

45 Petersen, 'Elettorato e base sociale del fascismo italiani negli anni venti', cit., p.649

46 Mauro Canali, *Le spie del regime*, Il Mulino, Bologna 2004, p.33

47 The circumstantial evidence can be found in ibid.

48 Mussolini, *Scritti politici*, cit., p.235

49 Lupo, *Il fascismo*, cit., p.185

50 Candeloro, *Il Movimento Cattolico in Italia*, cit., p.506

51 See cable from Mussolini instructing the Treasury to do everything possible to save the Banco di Roma in G. Guarino and G. Toniolo (eds), *La Banca d'Italia e il sistema bancario 1919–1936*, Laterza, Roma-Bari 1993, p.330n

52 Bosworth, 'The British Press, the Conservatives and Mussolini 1920–34', cit., pp.169–73

53 Joseph M. Hernon, Jr, 'The Last Whig Historian and Consensus History: George Macaulay Trevelyan, 1876–1962' in *The American Historical Review*, Vol. 18, No. 1, January–February 1976, pp.79–80

54 Gramsci, *Selections from the Political Writings 1921–1926*, cit., p.276

55 Marla Stone, 'Staging fascism: The Exhibition of the Fascist Revolution' in *Journal of Contemporary History*, Vol. 28, No. 2, 1993, pp.215ff

# BIBLIOGRAPHY OF WORKS CITED

Abse, Tobias, 'Italian Workers and Italian Fascism' in Richard Bessel
(ed.), *Fascist Italy and Nazi Germany*, CUP 1996

Adamson, Walter L., *Avant-garde Florence. From Modernism to Fascism*, Harvard University Press 1993

Alatri, Paolo, *Le origini del fascismo*, Editori Riuniti, Roma 1977

Albanese, Giulia, 'Dire violenza, fare violenza. Espressione, minaccia, occultamento e pratica della violenza durante la Marcia su Roma' in *Memoria e Ricerca*, No. 13, May–August 2003

Araldi, Vinicio, *Camicie nere a Montecitorio: storia parlamentare dell'avvento del fascismo*, Mursia, Milano 1974

Arpaia, Paul, 'Constructing a national identity from a created literary past: Giosuè Carducci and the development of a national literature' in *Journal of Modern Italian Studies*, Vol. 7, No. 2, 2002

Balbo, Italo, *Diario 1922*, Mondadori, Milan 1932

Baldoli, Claudia, *Bissolati immaginario. Le origini del fascismo cremonese. Dal socialismo riformista allo squadrismo*, cremonabooks, Cremona 2002

Becker, Jean-Jacques, *1914: Comment les Français sont entrés dans la guerre*, Presses de la fondation nationale des sciences politiques, Paris 1977

Berta, Giuseppe, *Il governo degli interessi. Industriali, rappresentanza e politica nell'Italia del nord-ovest 1906–1924*, Marsilio, Venice 1996

Bidussa, David, *Il mito del bravo italiano*, il Saggiatore, Milan 1994

Bonadeo, Alfredo, *D'Annunzio and the Great War*, Fairleigh Dickinson University Press, Madison NJ 1995

Bosworth, Richard J.B., 'The British Press, the Conservatives and Mussolini 1920–34' in *Journal of Contemporary History*, Vol. 5, No. 2, 1970

Bosworth, Richard J.B., *The Italian Dictatorship. Problems and Perspectives in the Interpretation of Mussolini and Fascism*, Arnold, London 1998

Bosworth, Richard J.B., *Mussolini*, Arnold, London 2002

Bourke, Joanna, *Dismembering the Male. Men's Bodies, Britain and the Great War*, Reaktion Books, London 1996

Brustein, William, 'The "red menace" and the rise of Italian Fascism' in *American Sociological Review*, Vol. 56, No. 5, October 1991

Burgwyn, H. James, *The Legend of the Mutilated Victory: Italy, the Great War, and the Paris Peace Conference, 1915–1919*, Greenwood Press, Westport Conn. 1993

Canali, Mauro, *Le spie del regime*, Il Mulino, Bologna 2004

Canali, Mauro, *Il delitto Matteotti*, Il Mulino, Bologna 2004

Candeloro, Giorgio, *Il Movimento Cattolico in Italia*, Riuniti, Rome 1982

Candeloro, Giorgio, *Storia dell'Italia Moderna*, Vol. 6, Feltrinelli, Milan 1970

Candeloro, Giorgio, *Storia dell'Italia Moderna*, Vol. 8, *La Prima Guerra Mondiale. Il Dopoguerra. L'avvento del fascismo*, Feltrinelli, Milan 1984

Capacci, Giuseppe, *Diario di guerra di un contadino toscano*, Cultura editrice, Florence 1982

Cardoza, Anthony L., *Agrarian Elites and Italian Fascism. The Province of Bologna 1901–1926. The Province of Bologna 1901–1926*, Princeton University Press 1982

Carocci, Giampiero, *Il Trasformismo dall'unità ad oggi*, Unicopli, Milan 1992

Clark, Martin, *Mussolini*, Pearson Longman, Harlow 2005

Conti, Ettore, *Dal taccuino di un borghese*, Garzanti, Milano 1971

Corner, Paul, 'The Road to Fascism: an Italian *Sonderweg?*' in *Contemporary European History*, Vol. 11, No. 2, 2002

Corner, Paul, *Fascism in Ferrara 1915–1925*, OUP 1975

Crispi, Francesco, *Scritti e discorsi politici (1849–1890)*, Unione Cooperativa Editrice, Rome 1890

Croce, Benedetto, *Nuove pagine sparse*, Vol. 1, Riccardo Ricciardi editore, Naples 1949

Cunsolo, Ronald S., 'Libya, Italian Nationalism, and the Revolt against Giolitti' in *The Journal of Modern History*, Vol. 37, No. 2, June 1965

D'Attorre, Pier Paolo, *Novecento padano: l'universo rurale e la 'grande trasformazione'*, Donzelli, Rome 1998

De Felice, Renzo, *Mussolini il rivoluzionario 1883–1920*, Einaudi, Turin 1965

De Felice, Renzo, *Mussolini il fascista. La conquista del potere 1921–1925*, Einaudi, Turin 1966

De Grand, Alexander, *The Hunchback's Tailor. Giovanni Giolitti and Liberal Italy from the Challenge of Mass Politics to the Rise of Fascism, 1882–1922*, Praeger, Westport Conn. 2001

Detti, Tommaso, *Serrati e la formazione del partito comunista italiano*, Riuniti, Rome 1972

Diamandouros, P. Nikiforos, 'Greek Political Culture in Transition: Historical Origins, Evolution, Current Trends' in Richard Clogg (ed.), *Greece in the 1980s*, Macmillan, London and Basingstoke 1983

Duggan, Christopher, *Francesco Crispi*, OUP 2002

Dunnage, Jonathan, *The Italian Police and the Rise of Fascism: A case study of the province of Bologna 1897–1925*, Praeger, Westport Conn. 1997

Einaudi, Luigi, 'Sulla buona via' in *Corriere della sera*, 18 November 1922

Einaudi, Luigi, 'Discordia felice' in *Corriere della sera*, 22 October 1922

Elazar, Dahlia Sabina, 'Electoral democracy, revolutionary politics and political violence: The emergence of fascism in Italy, 1920–21', *British Journal of Sociology*, Vol. 51, No. 3, September 2000

'L'esercito nei giorni della "Marcia su Roma": dalle memorie storiche della 16ª Divisione di Fanteria di stanza a Roma nel 1922' in *Storia Contemporanea*, Vol. 15, No. 6, December 1984

Farneti, Paolo, *Sistema politico e società civile*, Edizioni Giappichelli, Turin 1971

Fewster, Colin J., 'A Question of Loyalty: Hugo von Hofmannsthal, Stendhal, D'Annunzio, and Italian Nationalism' in *Seminar: A Journal of Germanic Studies*, Vol. 42, No. 1, February 2006

Foot, John M., ' "White Bolsheviks"? The Catholic Left and the Socialists in Italy, 1919–1920' in *The Historical Journal*, No. 2, Vol. 40, 1997

Forsyth, Douglas J., *The Crisis of Liberal Italy. Monetary and Financial Policy, 1914–1922*, CUP 1993

Gay, Peter, *Freud*, Macmillan, London 1989

Gentile, Emilio, *L'Italia giolittiana 1899–1914*, Il Mulino, Bologna 1977

Gentile, Giovanni, *Che cosa è il fascismo. Discorsi e polemiche*, Vallecchi, Florence 1924

Giolitti, Giovanni, *Discorsi Parlamentari*, Vol. 2, Camera dei Deputati, Rome 1953

Giolitti, Giovanni, *Discorsi extraparlamentari*, Einaudi, Turin 1952

Gobetti, Piero, *Scritti politici*, Einaudi, Turin 1997

Gramsci, Antonio, *Selections from the Political Writings 1921–1926*, Lawrence and Wishart, London 1968

Gregory, Adrian, 'British "War Enthusiasm" in 1914. A Reassessment' in Gail Braybon (ed.), *Evidence, History and the Great War*, Berghahn Books, New York and Oxford 2003

Grisi, Francesco (ed.), *I futuristi*, Newton, Milan 1994

Guarino, G. and G. Toniolo (eds), *La Banca d'Italia e il sistema bancario 1919–1936*, Laterza, Roma-Bari 1993

Hernon, Jr, Joseph M., 'The Last Whig Historian and Consensus
    History: George Macaulay Trevelyan, 1876–1962' in *The
    American Historical Review*, Vol. 18, No. 1, January–February
    1976

Hitler, Adolf, *Mein Kampf*, Hutchinson, London 1969

Kant, Immanuel, *Observations on the Feeling of the Beautiful and
    Sublime*, trans. by John T. Goldthwait, University of California
    Press 1991

Kelikian, Alice, *Town and Country under Fascism. The
    Transformation of Brescia 1915–1926*, Clarendon Press, Oxford
    1986

Lenin, V.I., *Left-Wing Communism: an Infantile Disorder*, in *Collected
    Works*, Vol. 31, Progress Publishers, Moscow 1966

Levra, Umberto, 'Il Parlamento nella crisi di fine secolo' in *Storia
    d'Italia, Annali 17*, Einaudi, Turin 2001

Lupo, Salvatore, *Il fascismo. La politica in un regime totalitario*,
    Donzelli, Rome 2005

Lyttelton, Adrian, 'The "Crisis of Bourgeois Society" and the Origins
    of Fascism' in Richard Bessel (ed.), *Fascist Italy and Nazi
    Germany*, CUP 1996

Lyttelton, Adrian, *The Seizure of Power. Fascism in Italy 1919–1929*,
    Weidenfeld and Nicolson, London 1973, p.30

Mack Smith, Denis, *Italy. A Modern History*, Michigan University
    Press, Ann Arbor 1959

Mack Smith, Denis, *Italy and its Monarchy*, Yale University Press,
    New Haven and London 1989

Maier, Charles S., *Recasting Bourgeois Europe. Stabilization in France,
    Germany, and Italy in the decade after World War I*, Princeton
    University Press 1975

Mavrogordatos, George Th., *Stillborn Republic: Social Conditions and
    Party Strategies in Greece 1922–1936*, University of California
    Press, Berkeley Cal. 1983

Melograni, Piero, *Storia Politica della Grande Guerra*, Laterza, Bari
    1969

Melograni, Piero, *Gli industriali e Mussolini, rapporti tra Confindustria e fascismo dal 1919 al 1929*, Longanesi, Milan 1972

Milza, Pierre, *Mussolini*, Fayard, Paris 1999

Mondini, Marco, 'Between subversion and coup d'état: military power and politics after the Great War (1919–1922)' in *Journal of Modern Italian Studies*, Vol. 11, No. 4, December 2006

Montaldo, Silvano, 'Il Parlamento e la società di massa' in *Storia d'Italia, Annali 17, Il Parlamento*, a cura di Luciano Violante, Giulio Einaudi, Turin 2001

Morabito, Pierfrancesco, 'Movimenti artistici e società di massa: il futurismo italiano' in *Italia Contemporanea*, No. 150, March 1983

Mosca, Gaetano, *Sulla teorica dei governi e sul governo parlamentare*, Tipografia dello Statuto, Palermo 1884

Mosier, John, *The Myth of the Great War*, Profile Books, London 2001

Mosse, George L., 'The Two World Wars and the Myth of the War Experience' in *Journal of Contemporary History*, Vol. 33, No. 4, 1998

Mussolini, Benito, *Il mio diario di Guerra (1915–1917)*, Imperia, Milano 1923

Mussolini, Benito, *Scritti politici*, Feltrinelli, Milano 1979

Mussolini, Benito, *Opera Omnia*, edited by Edoardo and Duilio Susmel, La Fenice, Florence 1951–1963, Vols 4, 13, 14, 15, 18, 19

Nello, Paolo, *L'avanguardismo giovanile alle origini del fascismo*, Laterza, Roma-Bari 1978

Nitti, Francesco Saverio, *Peaceless Europe*, 1922 available on http://www.gutenberg.org/files/10090/10090-8.txt

Noiret, Serge, 'Il PSI e le elezioni del 1919. La nuova legge elettorale. La conquista del Gruppo parlamentare socialista da parte dei massimalisti', *Storia Contemporanea*, Vol. 15, No. 6, December 1984

O'Brien, Paul, *Mussolini in the First World War. The journalist, the soldier, the fascist*, Berg, Oxford 2005

Palla, Marco, 'La presenza del fascismo. Geografia e storia quantitativa' in *Italia Contemporanea*, No. 184, September 1991

*Parliamentary Papers*, London, 1920, LI Cmd. 671, Miscellaneous No. 7

*Partito nazionale fascista. Le origini e lo sviluppo del fascismo attraverso gli scritti e la parola del Duce e le deliberazioni del P.N.F., dall'intervento alla marcia su Roma*, Libreria del littorio, Roma 1928, preface by Augusto Turati

Petersen, Jens, 'Elettorato e base sociale del fascismo italiani negli anni venti' in *Studi Storici*, Vol. 16, No. 3, 1975

Pezzimenti, Alessandro, *L'avvento del fascismo attraverso le pagine del Corriere della sera (1919–1925)*, Tesi Università degli Studi di Milano, 2000–01, pp.13–15 accessed http://www.tesionline.com/intl/thesis.jsp?idt=6650

Piazzesi, Mario, *Diario di uno squadrista toscano 1919–1922*, Bonacci editore, Rome 1980

Pinkard, Terry, *Hegel. A Biography*, CUP 2000

Piretti, Maria Serena, *La giustizia dei numeri: Il proporzionalismo in Italia (1870–1923)*, Il Mulino, Bologna 1990

Preston, Paul, *Franco. A Biography*, HarperCollins, London 1993

Preti, Domenico, *Economia e istituzioni nello stato fascista*, Riuniti, Rome 1980

Procacci, Giovanna, 'Gli interventisti di sinistra, la rivoluzione di febbraio e la politica interna italiana nel 1917' in *Italia Contemporanea*, No. 138, 1980

Procacci, Giuliano, *La lotta di classe in Italia agli inizi del Secolo XX*, Riuniti, Rome 1978

Pugliese, Emanuele, *Io difendo l'esercito*, Rispoli, Naples 1946

Répaci, Antonino, *La marcia su Roma*, Rizzoli, Milan 1972

Riosa, Alceo, 'Le patriotisme dans le verbe' in proceedings of the conference *L'éloquence politique en France et en Italie de 1870 à nos jours*, Collection de l'École française de Rome, Rome 2001

Rizi, Fabio Fernando, *Benedetto Croce and Italian Fascism*, University of Toronto Press 2003

Robbins, Keith, *The First World War,* OUP 1984

Rocca, Massimo, *Come il fascismo divenne una dittatura. Storia interna del fascismo dal 1914 al 1925,* ELI, Milan 1952

Rossi, Mario G., 'Democrazia, socialismo, imperialismo nell'Italia giolittiana' in F. Andreucci et al. (eds), *Lezioni di storia d'Italia 1848–1948,* Riuniti, Rome 1979

Sabbatucci, Giovanni, *Il trasformismo come sistema,* Laterza, Roma-Bari 2003

Salandra, Antonio, *Memorie Politiche 1916–1925,* Garzanti, Milan 1951

Salvatorelli, Luigi and Giovanni Mira, *Storia d'Italia nel periodo fascista,* Einaudi, Turin 1956

Salvemini, Gaetano, *The Origins of Fascism in Italy,* Harper, New York 1973

Santomassimo, Gianpasquale, *La Marcia su Roma,* Giunti, Florence 2000

Segrè, Claudio G., *Italo Balbo. A Fascist Life,* University of California Press 1987

Serpieri, Arrigo, *La Guerra e le classi rurali italiane,* Laterza, Bari 1930

Snowden, Frank, *The Fascist Revolution in Tuscany, 1919–1922,* Cambridge University Press 1989

Spaventa, Silvio, 'Discorso contro la Conciliazione', 20 September 1886 in Valeri (ed.), *La lotta politica in Italia,* p.91

Spriano, Paolo, *Storia del partito comunista italiano. Da Bordiga a Gramsci,* Einaudi, Turin 1967

Spriano, Paolo, *The Occupation of the Factories,* Pluto Press, London 1975

Stone, Marla, 'Staging Fascism: The Exhibition of the Fascist Revolution' in *Journal of Contemporary History,* Vol. 28, No. 2, 1993

Strachan, Hew, *The First World War,* Vol. 1: *To Arms,* OUP 2001

Tardieu, André, *The Truth about the Treaty,* Boobs-Merrill Co., Indianapolis 1921, chapter three available at

http://www.lib.byu.edu/estu/wwi/comment/treatytruth/
tardieu00tc.htm

Tasca, Angelo, *Nascita e avvento del fascismo: l'Italia dal 1918 al 1922*,
Laterza, Bari 1967

Togliatti, Palmiro, 'Episodi della guerra civile in Toscana' in *Opere
1917–1926*, Vol. 1, Riuniti, Rome 1974

Togliatti, Palmiro, *Lectures on Fascism*, Lawrence and Wishart,
London 1976

Valeri, Nino, *D'Annunzio davanti al fascismo*, Le Monnier, Florence
1963

Valli, Roberta Suzzi, *Le origini del fascismo*, Carocci, Roma 2003

Veneruso, Danilo, *La vigilia del fascismo. Il primo ministero Facta
nella crisi dello stato liberale in Italia*, Il Mulino, Bologna 1968

Vivarelli, Roberto, *Il fallimento del liberalismo. Studi sulle origini del
fascismo*, Il Mulino, Bologna 1981

Vivarelli, Roberto, *Storia delle origini del fascismo: l'Italia dalla grande
guerra alla marcia su Roma*, Vol. 1, Il Mulino, Bologna 1991

Volpe, Gioacchino, *Guerra Dopoguerra Fascismo*, La Nuova Italia,
Venice 1928

Weber, Max, *Economy and Society. An outline of interpretative
sociology*, Vol. 1, University of California Press 1978

Zangheri, Renato, 'Introduction', *Lotte agrarie in Italia. La
Federazione nazionale dei lavoratori della terra 1901–1926*,
Feltrinelli, Milan 1960

# INDEX

Acerbo, Giacomo, 138
Adua, battle of (1896), 34
agricultural workers: unrest,
    90–1, 93
    conditions improved, 94
Albertini, Luigi: supports war on
    Libya, 34
    on Italian defeatism, 43
    co-founds Fascio nazionale di
    azione, 48
    ousted by Confindustria, 111
    condemns socialist
    'legalitarian' strike, 116
    detests Giolitti, 117, 131
    humiliated at banning of
    *Corriere della sera*, 137
    and murder of Matteotti, 139
    *see also Corriere della sera*
Alfonso XIII, King of Spain, 26
Ambris, Alceste de, 59
Amendola, Giovanni, 60, 134
Ansaldo (company), 52, 140
anti-clericalism, 113
Aosta, Emanuele Filiberto, Duca
    d', 131

Apulia, 97
Arbe (island), 59
Arditi, 48
army: support for fascists, 103,
    132
Associazione nazionale
    combattenti, 56
Associazione nazionalista
    italiana, 35
Austria (and Austro-Hungarian
    Empire): and nationalism, 31
    Italy declares war on (1915), 38
    Mazzini's hostility to, 41
    Vittorio Veneto defeat (1918),
    45
    empire dismembered (1918),
    49
    territories ceded to Italy, 54
*Avanti!* (newspaper), 41–3, 81

Balbo, Italo: on attaining power
    through violence, 9, 98
    opposes 1921 pact with
    socialists, 16, 105

Balbo, Italo – *cont.*
  and decision to march on
    Rome, 125
Banco di Roma, 140–1
Beccaris, General Bava, 78
Becker, Jean-Jacques: *1914:*
  *Comment les Français sont*
  *entrés dans la guerre*, 32
Beckmann, Max, 32
Belgium: wartime unity, 38
Benedict XV, Pope, 42, 113–14
Bergamo, 121
Bergson, Henri, 33
Bianchi, Michele, 117, 125
Bismarck, Prince Otto von, 123
Bissolati, Leonida, 41, 48, 62–3,
  80
Blackshirts (*camice nere*): in
  March on Rome (1922), 12
  attack Catholics, 114
  *see also* fascists, fascism
*blocco nazionale*, 90, 101
Bologna: local election successes
  (1920), 94
  support for fascism, 96
  fascist violence in, 97–8
Bolshevik Revolution (Russia,
  1917), 10
Bolzano, 115, 118
Bonaparte, Louis, 28
Bonomi, Ivanoè, 105, 113
Bordiga, Amadeo, 66
Bordighera, 14
Boselli, Paolo, 42
*braccianti* (day labourers), 90
Bresci, Gaetano, 129

Brescia, 95
Britain: wartime unity, 38
  maintains colonial empire after
    First World War, 49
  and Italian economy, 55
  as parliamentary democracy,
    68
  recognition of Mussolini, 141
Brooke, Rupert, 32
Buozzi, Bruno, 90

Cadorna, General Luigi, 42–3
Capacci, Giuseppe, 46
Capello, General Luigi, 48
Caporetto, battle of (1917),
  42–3, 45
*carabinieri*: support for fascists,
  102–3
Carducci, Giosuè, 35
*Carta di Carnaro*, 59
Case del popolo (socialist
  cultural circles): attacked by
  fascists, 98
Catholics: attitude to First
  World War, 33, 36, 42
  declare loyalty to state in war,
    38
  and Giolitti's reforms, 79–80,
    82
  and social change, 79
  and Giolitti's 1920
    government, 86
  among peasantry, 91
  Mussolini attempts to
    conciliate, 113

attacked by Blackshirts, 114
support Mussolini's government, 133
*see also* Church
Cavazzoni, Stefano: as Minister for Labour and Social Security, 16
Chambers of Labour: attacked by fascists, 98
Church (Catholic): relations with political parties, 113–14, 121
supports Mussolini's government, 133
fascist Concordat with (1929), 140
*see also* Catholics
Churchill, (Sir) Winston, 141–2
Cipriani, Amilcare, 18
class (social): and revolution, 24–5
and parliamentary representation, 74
and political repression, 75
struggle, 112
Clemenceau, Georges, 50–1
Communist International: formed (1919), 83
Communist Party of Italy: and rise of Mussolini, 27
origins, 66
formed (1921), 88, 121
and divisions on left, 94
in 1921 election, 103–4
and Mussolini's appointment to premiership, 134

on history, 143
Concordat (with Vatican), 140
Confederazione italiana de lavoro (CIL), 84
Confederazione italiana dell'industria (Confindustria industrialists), 80–1, 87, 106, 109–12
Confederazione nazionale dei sindicati fascisti, 140
conscription, 91
Consiglio nazionale dell'avanguardia studentesca, 100
Conti, Ettore, 109
Corner, Paul, 30
Corradini, Enrico, 35
*Corriere dells sera* (newspaper): on fascist rise to power, 10, 117–18
attitude to Mussolini, 15
and fascist march on Rome, 22, 130, 135
supports war on Libya, 34
on Italian defeatism, 43
publishes D'Annunzio poem, 57
supports D'Annunzio, 58, 60
on Mussolini's Udine speech (1922), 108
accepts fascist violence, 115–16
status, 116–17
wariness of socialist threat, 117
opposition to Giolitti, 131
banned (1922), 137

corruption (political), 63, 71
Costa, Andrea, 18
Craponne, Louis Bonnefon, 80
Cremona, 121, 125
Crispi, Francesco, 34, 48, 72–5, 123, 135
Croce, Benedetto: attitude to Mussolini, 17–18, 133
  attends fascist 1922 Naples conference, 127

*Daily Mail*, 141
Dalmatia, 49–52, 54
D'Annunzio, Gabriele, 19, 56–61, 63, 100, 123
Depretis, Agostino, 70–1, 73
*destra storica, la see* 'historical right'
Diaz, General Armando: as War Minister, 16
*Difesa, La* (newspaper), 89

Ebert, Friedrich, 20
eight-hour day, 83
Einaudi, Luigi, 81, 88, 108, 111, 124, 130, 137
elections *see* general elections
Elena (Jelena), Queen of Victor Emmanuel III, 129
Emergency Tariff Act (USA, 1921), 54
Emilia-Romagna, 93, 97
*Energie nove* (journal), 89

Ethiopia: Italian defeat in (1896), 34, 75

Facta, Luigi: and defence of Rome against Blackshirts, 12
  drafts state of emergency decree, 15, 127–8
  second government (1922), 118, 122, 131
  condemns fascist violence, 121
  first government falls (1922), 122
Facta, Maria, 122
Farinacci, Roberto, 16, 63, 125
farming, 90–2
Fasci di combattimento: programme, 61
  transformed into political party, 105
Fascio nazionale di azione, 48
Fascio parlamentare di difesa nazionale, 48
fascists, fascism: supporters, 4
  rise to power, 9–11, 118, 125, 133–4
  and March on Rome, 13–14, 22, 125–8, 131
  in coalition government (1922), 16
  early election failures, 19–20
  in Giolitti's national bloc (1921), 20
  Party membership numbers, 20

opponents suppressed, 21
Party loses importance as
  instrument of state, 21
political system, 22
origins, 29–30, 48, 62, 96
symbols, 47–8
early obscurity, 89
violence, 94–5, 97–8, 100–1,
  106, 114–16
alliance with landlords, 96,
  102
growth, 97
support in Trieste, 97
composition of membership,
  100–1
support from local police and
  *carabinieri*, 102–3
1921 election results, 103–5
party formed, 105–6
liberal economic policy,
  106–10
industrialists' view of, 109–11
break socialists' legalitarian
  strike, 112, 125
deny anti-clericalism, 113
actions tolerated by state, 116
nationalists' view of, 123, 125
Naples conference (1922),
  126–7
enter Rome, 135
state structures, 137
1924 landslide election victory,
  138
totalitarian legislation, 139–40
Federazione lavoratori della
  terra, 93

Federzoni, Luigi: as Minister
  for Colonies, 16
Felice, Renzo de, 89, 134
Ferrara, 95–6, 98
FIAT (car-maker), 52, 84, 88
Finzi, Aldo, 136
FIOM (engineering workers'
  union), 90
Fiume: Italian dispute with
  Yugoslavia over, 50–2, 54
  D'Annunzio in, 57–9
  Italy granted sovereignty, 59,
    140
  recognised as free city, 59
  fascist violence in, 97
food prices, 77–8, 83
food rationing: in wartime,
  91
Fordney McCumber Tariff
  Act (USA, 1922), 54
Forsyth, Douglas, 82
France: and outbreak of First
  World War, 32
  wartime unity, 38
  maintains colonial empire
    after First World War, 49
  and political parties, 68
  state strength, 68
  labour movement suppressed,
    85
Franco, General Francisco, 29
Franz Ferdinand, Archduke of
  Austria, 31
Freikorps (Germany), 20
Freud, Sigmund, 32
futurists, 35, 58, 62, 123

Garibaldi, Giuseppe, 68
general elections: (1913), 36
  (1919), 64–5, 93–4
  (1921), 19–20, 98, 103–4
  (1924), 138
Genoa: industrial unrest, 85
Gentile, Giovanni: and March
  on Rome, 10
Gentiloni, Vincenzo Ottorino,
  79
Germany: post-First World War
  political violence, 20–1
  wartime unity, 38
  defeat in First World War, 49
  political parties in, 68
  unification, 68
  Crispi takes as state model, 73
  labour movement suppressed,
  85
Giolitti, Giovanni: and
  Mussolini's accession to
  power, 10
  and 1921 election, 19–20, 103
  and war on Libya, 34–5
  reluctance to enter First World
  War, 36
  supports state in war, 40
  and proposed negotiated
  peace, 48
  and economy, 54
  removes D'Annunzio from
  Fiume, 59
  blamed for corruption, 63
  rise to power, 75
  economic/social reforms,
  76–82, 122

and rise of trade unions, 76
widens suffrage, 76
courts Catholic support, 79–80
industrialists turn against,
  80–1, 110
and socialist opposition, 82–3
mediates in industrial unrest,
  85–7
forms 1920 government, 86
abolishes subsidy on bread, 87
includes fascist candidates in
  electoral lists (*blocco
  nazionale*), 90, 101–2
loses support of rural
  landowners, 96
unable to contain fascist
  violence, 103
fascists oppose in 1921
  parliament, 104
abolishes tax anonymity, 111
Catholics oppose, 114
Albertini's hostility to, 117
negotiates with Mussolini, 124
as Victor Emmanuel III's
  prime minister, 129
and fascist march on Rome,
  130
declines appointment to
  premiership (1922), 131
as 'dictator', 135
and Mussolini's electoral law,
  138
condemns Grand Fascist
  Council's power to list
  parliamentary candidates,
  140

Giuriati, Giovanni: as minister, 16

Gobetti, Piero, 89

*La Rivoluzione liberale*, 124

Gramsci, Antonio, 27, 43, 66, 89, 97, 143

Grand Fascist Council: forces Mussolini to resign, 11

powers, 140

Grandi, Dino: opposes pact with socialists, 16, 105

and Salandra's declining premiership, 129

Greece: political corruption, 71

Hardie, Keir, 33

Hardinge, Sir Charles, Baron, 51

Hegel, Georg Wilhelm Friedrich, 25

'historical left' (*la senestra storica*), 70, 84

'historical right' (*la destra storica*), 69–70, 73, 84

Hitler, Adolf: and outcome of World War II, 29

*Mein Kampf*, 32

Hofmannsthal, Hugo von, 32

industrialists *see* Confederazione italiana dell'industria

*Instaurare Omnia in Christo* (Pius X), 79

*Intransigeant, L'* (Paris newspaper), 35

Italia Nostra (organisation), 40

Italy: coalition government (1922), 16

and establishment of fascist dictatorship, 23–5

reluctance to enter First World War, 33–4, 38

colonial empire, 34–5, 75

nationalism, 34–6

attitudes to First World War, 37–43

enters war (1915), 37–8

expectation of post-war territorial gains, 37, 49–51, 54

divided views on war, 38–9

political apathy, 40

effect of First World War on, 45–7

war casualties, 45, 49

and end of First World War, 49

and peace negotiations, 50–1

post-war economic and industrial decline, 52, 54–5

remittances from Italians abroad, 54–5

'war' party dominates, 56–7

parliament's status and composition, 63–6, 68–74, 83, 86, 104–5, 112

suffrage, 66, 76, 79

constitution, 67, 69

weak post-war governments, 67

unification, 68–9

Italy – *cont.*
  political corruption, 71
  lack of political parties, 72–3
  industrial unrest, 77–8, 85, 88, 93
  average income, 78
  social conflicts, 78, 82, 84–5
  state welfare, 79
  industrial development under Giolitti, 82
  social progress, 82
  emigration, 90
  economic growth (1921–5), 111
  demands for strong government, 118–20
  Chamber abolished (1934), 130
  1923 electoral law (*legge Acerbo*), 138
  foreign policy under fascists, 140–1
  economy stabilised, 141
  life under fascist rule, 142
  *see also* general elections

Japan: defeats Russia (1905), 31
Juárez, Benito: Mussolini named for, 18

Kant, Immanuel, 34
Kipling, Rudyard, 32
Kuliscioff, Anna, 135

Labour Party (British): and outbreak of First World War, 33
Lampedusa, Tommaso de: *The Leopard*, 25
Land Leagues, 98
land reform, 83, 90–3
*Lavoratore di Trieste, Il* (newspaper), 97
leaseholders (*affittuari*), 90
Lenin, Vladimir I.: on revolution, 24, 84
  and Italian communist boycott of 1919 election, 83
  and Third International, 121
Leo XIII, Pope, 79
Liberals: general election losses (1919), 64, 66, 84
  and *trasformismo*, 70
  divided, 86
  local election losses (1920), 94
  and prospective alternative government to socialists, 122
  weakness, 124–5
  and fascist march on Rome, 130
  support Mussolini's government, 133–4
Libya: Italy occupies, 34–5
Liebknecht, Karl, 21
Lloyd George, David, 51
Lollis, Cesare de, 40
Lombardy, 93
London, Treaty of (1915), 38, 49–50, 52

Luxemburg, Rosa, 21
Lyttelton, Adrian, 54, 103

MacDonald, Ramsay, 33
Malagodi, Olindo, 51
*Manchester Guardian*:
    Mussolini's interview in, 110,
    127
Mann, Thomas, 32
Mantua, 98
Manzoni, Alessandro, 34
Margherita, Queen Mother, 14
Marinetti, Emilio Filippo
    Tommaso, 35, 62, 123
Marx, Karl, 28
Matteotti, Giacomo, 111, 122,
    139
maximalists, 66–7, 83, 86, 88, 94,
    120–3, 132
Mazzini, Giuseppe, 41
Menelik, Emperor of Ethiopia,
    34
Miglioli, Guido, 121
Milan: fascist movement formed
    in, 62
  industrial unrest, 85
  fascist violence in, 115
  Mussolini's speech (4 October
    1922), 115
  local elections (1922), 121
  calm on Mussolini's
    appointment to premiership,
    133
Minghetti, Mario, 70–1
Missiroli, Mario, 102

monarchy: Mussolini cooperates
    with, 11–12, 112
  radical fascists oppose, 22
  constitutional powers, 67, 69,
    72
Mondini, Marco, 132
Mosca, Gaetano: *Sulla teorica dei
    governi e sul governo
    parlamentare*, 68–9
Mosse, George, 47
Mostra della rivoluzione fascista
    (Exhibition of the Fascist
    Revolution, 1932), 143
Mussolini, Alessandro (BM's
    father), 18, 63
Mussolini, Arnaldo (BM's
    brother), 139
Mussolini, Benito: accession to
    premiership, 9–11, 15–17,
    22–4, 29–30, 122, 129, 133–6
  arrives in Rome (October
    1922), 9, 12, 14–15, 22, 112
  cooperates with monarchy,
    11–12, 112
  dismissed legally, 11
  compromises with legality, 15
  social/family background,
    17–19, 63
  First World War service, 18–19
  maintains continuity of
    policies, 22
  old elite's expectations of, 25
  image, personality and
    achievements, 28, 143
  on belligerence of military
    chaplains, 42

Mussolini, Benito – *cont.*
  expelled from PSI, 43
  supports First World War,
    43–4
  anti-parliamentarianism, 63–4
  rhetoric, 63
  economic policies, 82
  industrialists' *rapprochement*
    with, 87, 109–11
  uncertain early aims, 89
  forms fascist movement, 96
  supported by landowners, 96
  praised in Trieste, 97
  and rural support, 97
  in 1921 parliament, 104–6
  forms and leads fascist political
    party, 105–6
  pact with socialists (1921), 105
  declares fascist programme,
    106–8
  anti-state tirade, 108–9
  interviewed in *Manchester
    Guardian*, 110, 127
  attempts to conciliate Church,
    113
  recognised as respectable
    statesman, 114–15
  foreign policy, 123
  welcomed by conservatives,
    123–4
  announces march on Rome,
    125–6
  and offer of premiership to
    Salandra, 130
  dictatorial rule and powers,
    136–9, 142

  inaugural speech (16
    November 1922), 136–7
  justifies violence, 139
  Pope praises, 140
  international recognition of,
    141
  historical place, 142


Naples: fascist conference
    (1922), 112, 126–7
Napoleon I (Bonaparte),
    Emperor of the French, 25
Napoleon III, Emperor of the
    French (*earlier* Louis
    Napoleon), 26
nationalism: rise of, 31
  in Italy, 34–6
  and rise of fascism, 123
Nazis: blame betrayal for
    wartime defeat, 38
Nicola, Enrico de, 127, 130
Nitti, Francesco Saverio: policy
    of post-war reconstruction, 5,
    55–6
  succeeds Orlando as Prime
    Minister (1919), 52
  and D'Annunzio's expedition
    to Fiume, 58
  sends good wishes to
    D'Annunzio after injury, 60
  on composition of parliament,
    64
  depends on PPI for support, 84
  and Giolitti's appointment as
    Prime Minister, 86

policy on social spending, 87
loses support of rural
  landowners, 96
demands strong government,
  118–19
and prospective reforms, 122

Ordine nuovo (group), 66
Organizzazione di vigilanza
  repressione dell'antifascismo
  (OVRA: Special Tribunal
  for the Defence of the State),
  140
Orlando, Vittorio Emanuele, 47,
  50, 54–5
Ottoman Empire: collapse, 31
  Italy declares war on
  (1911–12), 34
Oviglio, Aldo: as Minister of
  Justice, 16

*pacificazione, patto di* (1921), 16
pacifism, 33
Páez, Jose Antonio, 26
Papini, Giovanni, 44
Paris peace conference
  (1918–19), 50–1, 54
Partito populare italiano (PPI):
  founded, 19, 42, 80
  growth, 61
  general election success (1919),
    64–5, 84
  electoral discipline and control,
    66

non-cooperation with
  socialists, 67, 84
support for land reform, 92
local election successes (1920),
  93
general election results (1921),
  103–4
divisions, 113, 122
Mussolini reassures, 113
relations with Vatican, 113–14
and proposed government of
  national unity, 120
Partito socialista italiano (PSI):
  Mussolini's 1921 pact with,
    16, 105
  represents urban workers, 19
  attitude to First World War,
    33, 36, 38, 43
  Bissolati in, 41
  expels Mussolini, 43
  post-war election successes, 61,
    64
  Mussolini criticises, 62
  electoral discipline and control,
    66
  cooperation with liberals, 67
  non-cooperation with Catholic
    PPI, 67, 84
  advance to strength, 77–8
  and worker representation,
    78–9
  and Giolitti's reforms, 80, 82
  Bologna Congress (1919), 83
  and industrial unrest, 87
  Communists split from (1921),
    88

Partito populare italiano – *cont.*
  peasant and rural hostility to,
    91, 93, 95
  local election successes (1920),
    93–4
  fascist violence against, 98
  unpopularity in Bologna, 98
  general election losses (1921),
    103–4
  calls for strike for return to
    legality, 116, 125
  and proposed government of
    national unity, 120–1
  division and split, 121–2
Partito socialista riformista, 62
Partito socialista unitario, 122
peasantry: Catholicism, 91
  hostility to PSI, 91, 93, 95
  *see also* land reform
Pelloux, Luigi, 123
Piedmont, 93, 123
  Statute of (1848), 67
Pilsudski, Marshal Józef, 26
Pirelli (company), 52
Pittaluga, General Vittorio, 57
Pius X, Pope, 79
Pius XI, Pope, 114, 140
Po Valley, 93–4, 96
police: support for fascists,
    102–3
  Mussolini purges, 139
*Popolo d'Italia, Il* (newspaper):
  on fascist rise to power, 10
  pro-war stance, 44
  importance to Mussolini,
    61–2

financial difficulties, 106
  Mussolini's anti-state tirade in,
    108
  publishes regulations of
    Milizia, 118
  on Mussolini's 1922 Cremona
    speech, 126
Portugal: dictatorship collapses
    (1974–5), 23
Prampolini, Camillo, 67
Prezzolini, Giuseppe, 44
Primo de Rivera, Miguel, 26
Princip, Gavrilo, 31
proportional representation:
  abolished (1925), 21, 138
  introduced (1919), 66
protectionism, 82
Prussia, 68, 123
Puccini, Giacomo, 60
Pugliese, General Emanuele:
  organises defence of Rome
    (1922), 12–13, 132

Raimondi, Antonio, 115
Rapallo, Treaty of (1920), 59
Ravenna, 98
reformists: among socialists,
    66–7, 80, 83, 94
Reggio Emilia, 94
*Rerum Novarum* (papal
    Encyclical), 113
*Resto del Carlino, il* (newspaper),
    102, 113
Revel, Tahon di, 132
revolution: conditions for, 24–5

Rhodes, 34
Rilke, Rainer Maria, 32
Risorgimento, 41, 48, 54, 69
Rocco, Alfredo, 140
Rome: March on (October
    1922), 9–15, 22, 101, 106,
    117–18, 125–7, 131
  defended against Blackshirts,
    12–13
  fascists enter, 135
  Treaty of (1924), 140
Rosas, Juan Manuel de, 26
Rossi, Cesare, 116
Rudini, Antonio, 75
rural bourgeoisie, 90–1
Russia: defeated by Japan
    (1905), 31

Salandra, Antonio, 36–7, 42, 47,
    86, 116, 129–30, 139
Salvatorelli, Luigi, 133
Salvemini, Gaetano, 41, 81, 135
Santa Anna, Antonio de, 26
Sarajevo: assassination (1914),
    31
*senestra storica, la see* 'historical
    left'
Serratti, Giacinto, 121
sharecroppers (*mezzadri*), 83,
    90–3
Social Democratic Party
    (Germany), 33, 67
Socialist party (Italy) *see* Partito
    socialista italiano
Sonnino, Sidney, 36–7, 49, 54

Soviet Union: dictatorship
    collapses (1989–91), 23
Spain: dictatorship collapses
    (1975–7), 23
Spaventa, Silvio, 73–4
Special Tribunal for the Defence
    of the State, 21, 140
*squadristi*, 16, 20, 89, 94–5
*Stampa, La* (newspaper), 116,
    133
Stefani, Alberto de: appointed
    Finance Minister, 16, 111,
    133
strikes (industrial), 77–8, 85, 88,
    93
students: support for fascists,
    100–1
Sturzo, Don Luigi, 42, 86, 120,
    122

Tangorra, Vincenzo: as Treasury
    Minister, 16
Tardieu, André, 50
Tasca, Angelo, 66
Thaon di Revel, Admiral Paolo:
    as Navy Minister, 16
Theses of Rome (March 1922),
    27
Third International, 121
Togliatti, Palmiro: on growth of
    fascist dictatorship, 21
  first mention of fascist threat,
    89
  on continuing class struggle,
    112

trade unions: Mussolini
   abolishes, 21, 25, 112
and industrial unrest, 24, 84–5,
   88
and outbreak of First World
   War, 33
and rise of patriotism, 43
and decline of *trasformismo*, 74
formed, 75–6
relations with state, 77
opposed by industrialist
   entrepreneurs, 81
and Giolitti's reforms, 82
organisation, 84
and agricultural workers, 93,
   96
*trasformismo*, 68, 70–2, 74–5, 80,
   86
Trentino, 37, 41, 49, 54
Trento, 51, 115, 118
Trevelyan, George Macaulay,
   141–2
Trieste, 37, 41, 49, 97
Turati, Filippo: attitude to
   entering war, 43
and Socialist Party reformism,
   66–7, 80, 83
and Socialist representation,
   79
declines to support Giolitti, 80,
   83, 86
criticises maximalists, 88
and prospective coalition
   government, 120–1
heads Partito socialista
   unitario, 122

Turin: working-class agitation,
   84–5
Turkey *see* Ottoman Empire
Tuscany, 93–4, 97–8
Tyrol, Cisalpine, 49

Udine: Mussolini's speech
   (1922), 108, 112, 117
Umberto I, King of Italy, 128–9
Umbria, 94, 97
Unione elettorale cattolica,
   79–80
Unione italiana del lavoro
   (UIL), 84
United States of America: as
   victor in First World War,
   49
and post-war settlement, 50
supports Yugoslavia, 50
economic dominance, 52, 54
immigration barriers, 54–5
and Italian economy, 55

Vecchi, Cesare Maria de, 129
Veglia (island), 59
Venetia, 93
Veneto, 98
Versailles, Treaty of (1919), 50
Victor Emmanuel II, King of
   Italy, 128
Victor Emmanuel III, King of
   Italy: appoints and dismisses
   Mussolini, 11, 15–16, 129,
   133

refuses to sign state of
emergency decree, 15,
127–32
qualities, 128–9
accession, 129
marriage, 129
fear of threat from left, 132
Vittorio Veneto, battle of
(1918), 45
Vivarelli, 56
Volpe, Gioacchino, 17

Weber, Max, 28, 32
Weimar Republic, 20, 67
Wilson, Woodrow, 48, 50–2,
54, 63
working class: co-option into
capitalism, 75
party representation, 78
agitation, 84–5, 87–8
organisations, 84
World War I: Mussolini's service
in, 18–19

and rise of fascism, 29
outbreak, 31–3
Italy's reluctance to enter,
33–4, 36
Italian attitudes to, 37–43
Italy enters (1915), 37
effect on Italy and Italians,
45–7
Woodrow Wilson urges
negotiated peace, 48
ends, 49
peace settlement, 50, 54
effect on Italian parliament, 64

Yugoslavia: formed, 50, 52
granted Zara, 59
and Treaty of Rome (1924),
140

Zanardelli, Giuseppe, 75
Zara, 52, 59
Zweig, Stefan, 32